Transformations

Transformations

By the Editors of Time-Life Books

TIME-LIFE BOOKS, ALEXANDRIA, VIRGINIA

CONTENTS

The Oneness of All Life

Living in a forested world at the edge of an abundant sea, the Indians of the Pacific Northwest felt a kinship with the life surrounding them. In this, they shared with humankind's earliest members the view that nature was but a disguise, hiding within the faces of its diverse forms one animating spirit.

Blessed by the gifts of their environment, including a seemingly endless food supply, the local tribes—the Tlingit, Tsimshian, Haida, Kwakiutl, Nootka, and others—had the free time in which to evolve a rich culture. That culture expressed in its diverse rituals and art—especially in wood carvings such as the ones shown on these pages—the interconnectedness of humans and animals. Linked body, mind, and soul to nature, these Indians had no trouble accepting the idea that through magical means a person could turn into an animal or that a bird, beast, or fish could become a human, a notion

once common to many peoples of the world. Nor did they have difficulty acknowledging that humans and animals were descended from common ancestors. In fact, they saw themselves as having animal forebears. Thus each of their clans—or groups of families—and in some cases each individual family, had its own animal totem, a kind of beneficent mascot requiring propitiation to preserve the group's good.

But the relationship between humans and other living beings, here and elsewhere, had its dark side. Owls and land otters terrified the Northwest Indians because those creatures were thought to house spirits of the dead; some people were believed to undergo horrible transformations into land otters. And as this book will show, in other parts of the world—even, in certain places, to this day—humans have been thought to transform into animal forms to serve evil purposes.

Totem poles create an imposing skyline in this nineteenth-century photograph of the Haida village of Masset, located in the Queen Charlotte Islands off British Columbia. High-hatted figures known as watchmen sit atop some of the poles. Read from top to bottom, such poles generally featured first the animal totem of the clan chief who raised the monuments, followed by figures that related to episodes in the clan's ancestral history. Here, some poles serve as house posts, helping to support the buildings' crossbeams while proclaiming the supernatural lineage of the inhabitants at the same time.

Totem Ties That Bind a Clan

A genealogy in wood, this Tsimshian totem pole in which wolves are the principal totems served as aide-mémoire of one family's lore. At the top, with his tail curled around his back, is a wolf, harking back to the time when the family migrated to its present location and a child was killed by a wolf.

The next two figures, a person and a wolf, commemorate the brother of the pole owner. According to the story, the boy was spirited away by the wolf whose tail he is clutching.

Appearing next is a bear—a special crest that belongs to the family. The bear is split down the middle, and the wolf carved below it seems to be biting the trailing end of the bear's spiraling intestines. The creatures symbolize a now-forgotten episode in the family mythology.

Twelve humanlike figures encircle an opening, near the base of the pole, that is large enough for a person to crawl through. Known as the Hole through the Sky, the opening at one time functioned as an entrance to the family's house. Ladders led up to the hole from both the inside and outside of the house.

Although the tribes of the Pacific Northwest became known to the world by names based on language groups, such as Tlingit and Nootka, their members referred to themselves by their clan names—Bears or Frogs or Killer Whales or whatever creature was the particular group's principal totem.

Belonging to a clan had its privileges. Like an extended family, the individuals within the group were closely connected to one another by their shared identification with the totem. They were also linked spiritually through the totem to a supernatural being in that animal form who, according to the clan's history, bestowed on their early ancestors certain rights— including the right to invoke the totem, perform a ritual dance, and wear a special mask. In addition, they would have better luck than competitors when hunting the totem animal, since as kin it would favor them over others.

Not surprisingly, totemism ruled the Indians' ceremonial life and art. The treasured animal myths were acted out by masked dancers at elaborate hospitality festivals called potlatches. And the great totem poles and the family masks representing the totem animals were regularly commissioned and used to exalt a clan's supernatural lineage. Even common utensils might bear totems. All such objects, monumental and mundane, served as reminders of a clan's animal ties and of the debt owed nature for its munificence.

*A Kwakiutl mask of many faces appears outwardly to be a fish known
as a bullhead (top), but opens into a raven (bottom, left), and then into a human
(bottom, right). The wearer could thus quickly transform himself from
one ancestral figure into another during a totemic ceremony.*

Invoking the Spirits

Animals may have looked like animals to the Indians of the Pacific Northwest, but tradition taught that they were essentially humans in bestial skins, who permitted themselves to be killed in order that tribes might consume their flesh and flourish. So great a sacrifice could not go unrewarded; it demanded that the Indians not only honor their benefactors but also follow careful rituals to ensure that the creatures would continue to regard them favorably. The bones of their staple food, the migratory Pacific salmon, thus had to be burned or thrown into the sea in the hope that the salmons' souls might spread word among the salmon hordes of how respectfully this year's catch had been treated by the fishermen. The grateful fish could then be expected to come back the next year in numbers.

Similarly, a slain bear would be brought into the house, formally greeted, and given the respect due an important guest. If they venerated it, they reasoned, the bear's spirit would surely persuade other bears to visit the village. But woe to those who insulted the bear's spirit or denied it proper formalities. The spirit might punish the village by avoiding it, thus depriving the people of bear meat and skins.

Carved figures such as the ones above were probably used by shamans, or medicine men, during salmon rites to invoke the spirits of the fish and ensure a good catch. All these objects once belonged to a Tsimshian shaman.

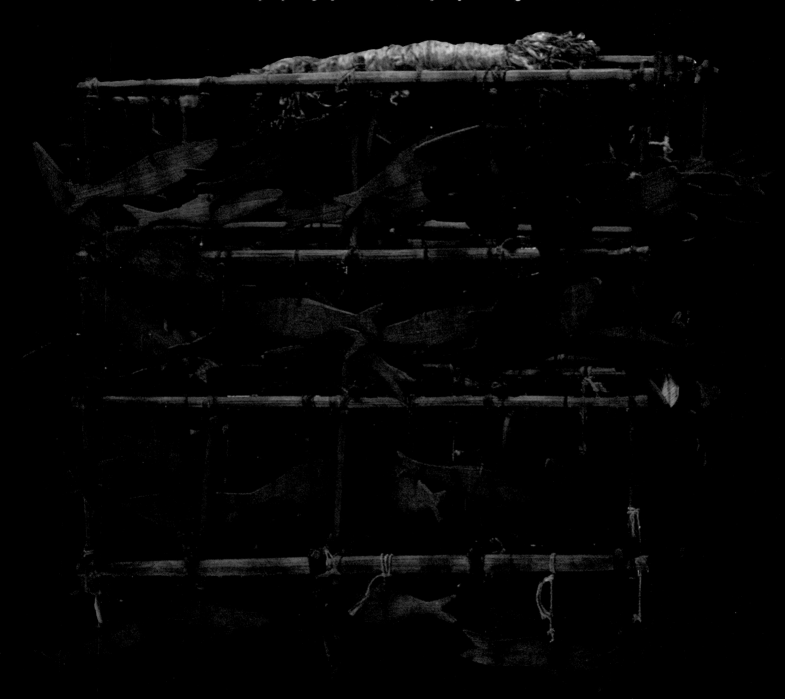

Dozens of small carved fish dangle from a cagelike frame-
work in this Nootka shaman's rattle. Such rattles were used in dances
before fishing expeditions to entreat fish spirits to be generous.

A salmon reveals its human soul in the Tlingit wooden sculpture at left. In addition to
the human head emerging from the gaping
mouth, there is an arm tucked beneath
the fin and the tail is splitting into two legs.

Masks of the Shadow World

Thanks to the bounty they accumulated during the busy spring and summer and laid away for the winter, the Indians of the Pacific Northwest could settle down in their great community houses when the weather turned cold and tend to their religious needs. During this ceremonial season of howling winds and thundering storms, supernatural spirits were deemed unusually close at hand.

To honor and to celebrate the spirit world—and to entertain themselves during those inclement days and long nights—clans staged enactments of their ancestral myths, using masks that were carved with the images of their totems.

Lit only by the flickering firelight, the masked performers seemed to their audiences to be physically transformed into animals or supernatural spirits. Often the dancers themselves felt taken over by the very creature whose mask hid their own features. The raven mask shown here, like the masks that are displayed on the following pages, is a powerful symbol of the tenuous line separating humans from other beings.

Unmistakably avian, yet eerily human, this Kwakiutl mask has a hinged beak that opened and shut with a clacking noise during dances. The half-bird, half-human appearance of the mask reflects the legendary ability of Raven—a supernatural creator being—to transform himself from bird to person.

Complete with tentacles, this Kwakiutl family-crest mask represents a giant octopus. By manipulating the strings, a performer could make the tentacles pulsate. He could also open and shut the mask's lower mouth, reinforcing the impression that the animal's spirit truly possessed the performer.

The tail, fins, and mouth of this Kwakiutl killer-whale mask—which is several feet long—all move. Killer whales were considered the most powerful of the Ocean People, supernatural beings thought to live as humans in villages under the sea.

The spirit Sisiutl, a fierce double-headed serpent linked with warrior power and invulnerability, is depicted in this Kwakiutl mask. The stylized human face in the center may symbolize the Indian warrior, who is able to summon Sisiutl on command. The tongues of the serpents are retractable.

A Tlingit shaman wore this wolf mask to reflect the wolf spirit that he believed possessed him—and from whom he supposedly obtained his own otherworldly powers and wisdom.

Worn by the Tlingit in ceremonial dances, this owl mask was designed to strike terror into the audience. Owls, associated with the souls of the dead, were greatly feared by the Indians.

Two frogs crawl over the forehead of this Tlingit shaman's mask of a human face; another emerges from its mouth. The mask expresses the frog's duality, a human under an animal facade.

The Tlingit shaman's mask below exemplifies the fate that awaited the unfortunate person who got lost in the forest—a werewolflike transformation into a fearsome land-otter–man.

CHAPTER 1

The Animal Connection

Skin blackened, hair cropped short, and wearing only a leather loincloth, an Englishman called Frederick Kaigh settled on his perch in a tree as the dark shadows of the forest night gathered around him. He felt foolish. This was the 1930s, after all, and his getup would have been more suitable for a Victorian explorer on a romantic African adventure than for a twentieth-century man—a physician, in fact—even here in a remote region on the border of the Belgian Congo and Northern Rhodesia. But he knew that he must not be recognized; if the crowd assembling in the clearing near his tree became aware that a European was present, the secret dance that was about to begin would be halted.

With the appearance in the clearing of a *nyanga*, or witch doctor, the drums started beating "on a note and a rhythm I had not heard before," Kaigh later recalled. It was a rhythm that reverberated "inside one and tingled down the spine: a rhythm which seemed gradually to take on a bestial quality." To the accompaniment of the drums, the nyanga began a chant, answered by those seated in a ring on the ground. It grew louder and louder, fueled by the strong native beer being drunk by all present. Then rising to a high-pitched scream, the chant came suddenly to a halt, and an eerie silence filled the clearing.

The crouching nyanga was dressed as a jackal; skins of the animal hung from his body, which had been striped along the spine and across the ribs with white paint, and over his hair he wore the head of this doglike beast. Kaigh watched spellbound while the nyanga made medicine "in a little fire that burned with queer light as he threw his concoctions on the flames" and then drank a potion he had prepared. At the sound of a distant, faint jackal cry, the witch doctor stood up, jumped on the fire, and scattered the coals with his feet. From his mouth, "sudden as a gunshot," came the shrill, piercing howl of a beast, answered from the jungle by similar cries.

The witch doctor danced with ever increasing abandon, drawing upon an energy reserve that belied his advancing years, working himself into a frenzy and foaming at the mouth, until, exhausted, he dropped to the ground in an apparent trance. The hidden English spectator found the performance

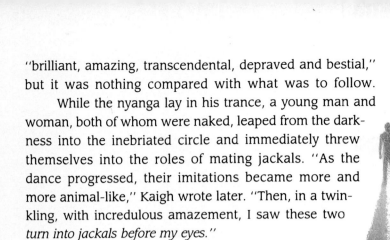

"brilliant, amazing, transcendental, depraved and bestial," but it was nothing compared with what was to follow.

While the nyanga lay in his trance, a young man and woman, both of whom were naked, leaped from the darkness into the inebriated circle and immediately threw themselves into the roles of mating jackals. "As the dance progressed, their imitations became more and more animal-like," Kaigh wrote later. "Then, in a twinkling, with incredulous amazement, I saw these two *turn into jackals before my eyes.*"

When he later related the experience in his book *Witchcraft and Magic of Africa,* Kaigh would ask himself: "Did it really happen?" He wondered whether he could have been the victim of mass hypnosis. Perhaps a hallucinogen had been introduced into the fire by the nyanga. But the thought also crossed Kaigh's mind that something supernormal may have occurred within the circle—that in becoming the human embodiment of the jackal, the witch doctor had somehow managed in the depth of his trance to project the animal's spirit into the young man and woman and thus turn them into beasts.

All Kaigh knew for certain was that he had witnessed an occurrence as old as humankind, the seeming ability of some specially gifted—or cursed—men and women to transform themselves or others into animals. There is even a word for it: *lycanthropy,* from the Greek *lukos* for wolf and *anthropos* for man. It is a belief that has persisted for centuries around the world, in cultures as diverse as those of Europe, Africa, India, China, Japan, and pre-Columbian America, and is at the heart of many myths, legends, and fairy tales. Among those individuals who have claimed to have witnessed transformations or to have turned into a beast, the mystery defies analysis. For those who have studied the phenomenon, lycanthropy is seen as a matter of illusion, delusion, or even madness, abetted often by the wearing of animal skins or the use of psychic stimulants, or both. Whatever its dynamics, lycanthropy was for so long so powerful a belief that it gave birth to two of the most fearsome of night creatures, the werewolf and the vampire.

If Kaigh's story were the only twentieth-century account of a transformation, it might be dismissed as nothing more than the distorted product of a febrile imagination, one that was perhaps overly stimulated by the rich lycanthropic literature of the past and the mysteries of Africa. But there are other chilling tales of transformations related by

modern eyewitnesses. A number of such accounts appeared in a 1918 edition of England's *Cornhill Magazine*, three of them from a British officer stationed in a remote district of northern Nigeria, which was then a British dependency. The author of the piece identified the officer only as Lieutenant F.

Many Nigerian locals believed that certain people possessed the power to change themselves under the cover of darkness into various beasts, including leopards and hyenas. Whether or not Lieutenant F was aware of this, at the time in question he was preoccupied with real animals, not transformations. For several nights running, something—hyenas, he believed—had been preying on his small collection of livestock, finally leaving him with only one sheep. To safeguard the survivor, he had it locked up in a hut. Around one in the morning he was wakened by the rustling of grass outside. He crept out into the darkness with his gun, prepared to shoot the intruder, but saw nothing and so returned to bed. No sooner had he dozed off than one of the locals came breathlessly into his room to announce that the last sheep had been killed by a hyena.

On entering the hut, the officer encountered a sickening scene. "The poor sheep was standing up," he wrote, "but its head was gone. The lower jaw only was whole, and stuck out in a horrible manner." He was convinced that the sheep's head had been cut away with a knife, but when he stepped outside and began searching for footprints, he found instead the tracks of a hyena.

The next night Lieutenant F set out a goat as bait and patiently waited for the marauder to return. Once again, about an hour after midnight, there was a disturbance and he saw something running toward the tethered animal. It was a hyena, all right. "It came with a rush, and stopped suddenly within two feet of the goat, spurting the gravel and sand almost into my face." The lieutenant raised his rifle and fired. Although "the brute fell head over heels," it managed to get up and make off. There was plenty of blood on the ground, but darkness prevented the lieutenant from immediately following the trail.

About twenty-five minutes after he shot the hyena, drums in the nearby village began to beat, "and the death-call rang through the air." At the time, the two events seemed unconnected.

In the morning, the lieutenant pursued the bloody spoor to a sandy place beside a stream, where the animal had paused to drink. Up to this point, the Englishman had followed hyena tracks, but now these were replaced by the prints of a man's bare feet. They led toward the village, then vanished where the morning's foot traffic had erased the trail. Afterward, the officer learned that the nocturnal drumbeats and wailing had marked the death of a prominent man in the village. Rumors said that he had died violently and that there had been a large wound in his body. But no one would admit to knowing the cause of it, and neither the Englishman nor his native servant was permitted to view the man's corpse.

The officer might have dismissed the wounding of the night visitor and the death in the village as mere coincidences had not the circumstances repeated themselves several days later. Having placed the carcass of a donkey in the bush as a lure for the hyenas, he sat on a tree branch with his rifle in hand and waited patiently for a scavenger to arrive. After two long, uneventful nights, he was too worn out to resume his post a third time, so he rigged up a gun trap that a prowler in the dark would trigger. At midnight the gun went off. Lieutenant F rushed from his house to investigate, but found nothing—and before long, he heard the death wail break out in the village.

By the light of morning, he tracked a trail of bloody paw prints to the settlement. They gave out not far from a house. He asked the villagers whether anyone had died the night before. Indeed, there had been a death—the mother of the village's chief—under circumstances as mysterious as they were sudden.

For a month afterward, as the officer noted, "I did

nothing to try to solve the question as to whether my nocturnal visitors were men, or beasts, or both." But when a horse died, providing bait, he saw his opportunity to make one more effort to get to the bottom of the mystery. He set up his gun trap near the carcass. On the second night, a shot rang out, followed by silence that lasted some half an hour. Then "the drumming started, and the cries of mourning for one just dead." And again, when the lieutenant followed the bloody spoor the next day, the hyena tracks dissolved into human footprints.

Undaunted, two nights later he once more rigged up his cocked rifle beside the horse and waited. The gun went off at one o'clock in the morning, and within twenty minutes, wailing began in another nearby village. This time the night visitor had been so severely wounded that it had dragged its legs as it retreated through the grass, leaving a crimson trail to the town. He learned from his servant the next day that two young men had died mysteriously on the nights his gun had fired. "There was nothing to account for their deaths," the lieutenant wrote, and as in the previous instances, he was denied access to the bodies. But no more hyenas came to the horse carcass, which was eventually consumed by vultures. Lieutenant F did not maintain that the visits by hyenas and the deaths in the villages offered proof in themselves of actual transformations having occurred, but if these were in fact merely coincidences, then by their timing and circumstances they were coincidences of a most unusual sort.

As an addendum to these stories, the *Cornhill* included the statement of a Captain H. H. Shott, who had been posted to Nigeria several years earlier. Shott had heard similar tales of the natives' ability to transform themselves but was deeply skeptical. After a large hyena had raided his camp for several nights running, he set his own trap for the beast. He tied a goat to a stake inside a thornbush zareba, or enclosure, and set up his cocked gun, with the barrel aimed straight at the entrance. For several nights, the hyena managed to make off with successive goats, without discharging the rifle. After discovering a weak place in the thornbush wall, through which the hyena apparently had gained access to the enclosure, Shott shifted the gun around, so that it now faced the hyena's entryway. And, indeed, that night the rifle went off, its bang followed instantly by the scream of a hyena in pain. Shott and a companion rushed in pursuit of the wounded animal. They could hear it thrashing about and moaning in the brush and, by the light of lanterns, were able to track it. They had not gone far when they found its jaw lying in a pool of blood. Despite its awful wound, the beast somehow managed to struggle on, to a village, where the trail went dead.

In the morning a delegation from the village came to see Captain Shott. They informed him that the *galadina,* one of their leaders, was dead and that Shott had killed him. The captain vehemently denied having shot anyone. "But you did shoot the galadina," the natives insisted, "only do not think that we mind. In reality we are rather glad, for we all know what the galadina was." And what he was, the grateful villagers explained, was a hyena-man, who wandered about under the cover of darkness in search of victims to satisfy his blood lust.

The delegation revealed the circumstances of the galadina's death: "Last night some of us saw the galadina going out of the town after sunset, and one of us asked him where he was going. The galadina said, 'I am going into the bush.' Now he always used to go into the bush about that time. Two hours later we heard your gun go off, and some time afterwards we saw the galadina come back. His head was all muffled up, and he walked like a very sick man. When he got to his compound, he drove out all his women, and this morning when we went to see him and to find out what was the matter he was lying dead, and his jaw was shot away." Shott was deeply shaken.

Even today, lycanthropy still has its firm believers. In Haiti, as the *Wall Street Journal* noted in a front-page story in 1988, a woman was arrested not long ago for supposedly turning children into animals and devouring them. And in Port-au-Prince, the country's capital, a man was reported to

A Jungle Cat-God Who Dwells Within

Since the dawn of humanity, animals have been revered and even worshiped throughout the world. The more powerful and predacious the beast, the more fear and respect it tends to elicit. In South and Central America, the dominant animal-deity has long been the jaguar. Even today for the region's Indians, the spotted cat commands awe as both a fearsome creature of the jungle and as a manifestation of the supernatural.

The jaguar shows its many otherworldly forms—from guardian of the gods to master of the air and beasts—in the art and lives of the people. The thousand-year-old statuette at right portrays a were-jaguar, born from the union of a jaguar and a mortal female. And the jaguar is key to the shamans' transformation rites. Through the careful use of narcotics, they allow the jaguar they say lies deep within to emerge. They then see themselves as jaguars and work their special magic, whether for prophecy, protection, or healing.

have been brutally hacked to death by machete-wielding assailants for being a werewolf. On the other side of the world, as the *Financial Times* of Britain reported in 1986, angry Malaysians beat a dog to death, convinced that it was a member of a gang of robbers who transformed themselves into animals to carry out their criminal acts.

The roots of these stories run deep. Indeed, they reach all the way back to the prehistoric caves of the Cro-Magnons in Spain and southern France, where among the 20,000- to 30,000-year-old paintings of animals that cover the walls may be found two of the earliest representations of *Homo sapiens.* Interestingly, these show the male not fully human, but as part animal. In one crudely drawn picture, a hunter lies on his back, perhaps in a trance like Kaigh's exhausted witch doctor, and his head is that of a bird and his hands are like claws. Close by is his spear, thought to be the implement that has just wounded a magnificent bison that stands on its last legs only inches away, its bowels hanging from its belly.

In the second image, a man with human beard, arms, and legs, but with the antlers and ears of a stag and the tail of a wolf or wild horse, appears to be taking a prancing step, perhaps a movement in a ritual dance. Found fifteen feet above the cave floor and at the end of a magnificently decorated chamber, this figure seems to preside over the assemblage of beasts that covers the walls. Why is he there? What purpose did the artists serve by showing men in animal guises? And what rites took place in these caves deep within the womb of the earth?

The answers can never be final, but thanks to information gathered over the years by a variety of researchers digging in the caves themselves, studying the artwork found

Located at the bottom of a hard-to-reach shaft in France's Lascaux Cave, this Cro-Magnon drawing offers a mystery, possibly of transformation: a man possessing birdlike features lying between a disemboweled bison and a bird.

there, and observing peoples in the wild, some informed guesses can be made. Curiously, the paintings and engravings often crop up in places that are inconvenient for viewing: in narrow niches, behind bulges in the rock, sometimes in areas that must have been not only difficult but also hazardous for the artists to work in. "It is simply impossible," says Johannes Maringer, a German archaeologist and student of prehistory, "that this art should have been invented, in these locations, to give pleasure to the eye of the beholder; the intention must always have been to veil it in mysterious secrecy."

What, then, were these ancient artists up to? According to Maringer and numerous other specialists, their art was a vehicle for magic—more specifically, for a form known as sympathetic hunting magic. Strong and intelligent, the Cro-Magnons were well-equipped with all kinds of weapons, from spears and stone knives to slings. Nevertheless, despite their impressive advantages, these early humans lived in a primitive world, always in the shadow of unpredictable and incomprehensible forces, which they

may have viewed as malign. Doubtless the hunters felt it imperative, through whatever means, to stave off misfortune, injury, and sometimes death, for some of the animals they came up against were extremely dangerous. Doubtless, too, they believed, like so many hunter-gatherers in remote parts of the earth today, that magic could assist them in dodging misfortune and in gaining control over the beasts they wished to kill.

By painting pictures of their prey on the walls of the caves the Cro-Magnons, in effect, strengthened their chances of dealing them a mortal wound during the hunt. Even at this juncture of the twentieth century, many isolated peoples around the world believe that creating the likeness of a person or a thing gives the creator some supernatural power over the subject. The artists may also have been thinking of their art as a kind of prayer, a way of ensuring that the beasts they so vividly limned on the rock surface would remain fertile, mate, and produce game that the hunters could then kill.

Hunting magic could explain the figures of men in an-

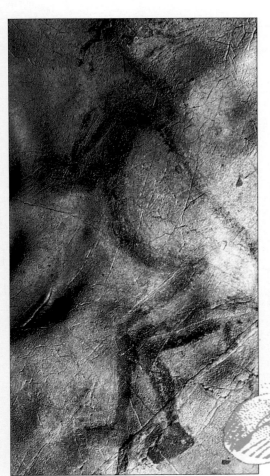

A painting of a purported sorcerer partially changed into a beast (above) covers part of a wall in les Trois Frères cave in France. The drawing at right, based on the original, shows human features, along with antlers and a bushy tail.

imal shapes also. They may be straightforward pictures of hunters disguised as animals and may have been intended to guarantee successful stalking. Or they may be more symbolic. Perhaps they were projections of the hunters' feeling that a painting showing a ritual dance by a magician or sorcerer either disguised as an animal or partly transformed into one would work more potent magic on the game. Around the figures of two bison discovered in one of the caves, for instance, the ghostly footprints of dancers turned up. Instead of pressing down on the soles of their feet as might be expected, these dancers tripped around on their heels and thus left hooflike impressions in the mud. Some scholars think that they were impersonating the bison, invoking the spirit of the animals through their own movements. They may also have been attempting to acquire some of the traits they would have most admired in bison, such as the animals' bullish strength and aggressiveness, attributes hunters needed to be successful.

Lycanthropy's origins thus lie in the dawn of civilization, when life for the human animal was brutish and short. Although at nature's mercy, our earliest ancestors doubtlessly felt themselves at one with the world, connected to all other living things. Most, if not all, probably did not see themselves as being superior to the animals, which, they recognized, possessed powers that they lacked. Nor did

they see themselves as being at the center of the universe, as humankind does today, but rather saw themselves only as a part of mother earth, dependent upon all its other parts for their survival. They belonged to nature and venerated everything from weather and water to the spirits in plants and animals. Whatever they took from the earth for their own well-being, they felt they had to give back, through gifts and sacrifices of like worth. "Their priests and worshippers lived upon this planet as its child, and not as an enemy or occupying force" is how one writer has put it.

Tuned into nature in ways that have long since been lost, these early humans learned to hunt disguised as the animals themselves—down on hands and knees, with skins draped over their backs. And to complete the illusion, they assumed the very qualities of their prey, emulating their movements and even their behavior, just as the Cro-Magnon dancers must have done as they danced before their bison effigies. Nevertheless, for all the wisdom they possessed, the hunters had much to fear. It is no wonder, then, that in an effort to gain still more cunning and strength, the hunters also sought to emulate those animals that were hunters themselves—wolves, bears, tigers, lions, and leopards.

Out of this respect for the creatures of wood and field grew a worldwide pattern of belief, in which humans and animals were seen as being intrinsically linked, having sprung from the same unknowable source. Even among the most primitive societies, apparently, the notion that all living things had an internal, incorporeal soul, as well as an external, physical form, flourished. In a world dominated by mystery and shadows, it was easy for people to assume that the soul left the body during dreams or trances and wandered about and in this detached state could enter another person or even an animal. And since, in their thinking, animals themselves had souls, it took no great leap of imagination to believe that the spirits of the beasts around them could invade their bodies as well. How easy, then, it would have been for people to accept the notion that men and women especially gifted at mimicking animals could turn themselves into animals and that the animals themselves could become humans. In a superstitious population, even mere talk of such transformations must have left a powerful impression on susceptible minds; indeed, lycanthropy would come to be regarded as a way of tuning into the world of spirit that underlay reality.

The kinship between human and animal was seen in some cultures as even more direct—individual people and beasts were thought to share a soul. An anecdote dramatically illustrates the point. Early in this century, a missionary in Africa, who was spending the night as a guest in a chief's hut, was aroused by a strange sound. It was made by a large, black, highly poisonous snake that was coiled and ready to strike. He reached for his rifle, but before he could fire at the reptile, the chief grabbed his arm and begged him not to shoot. The snake, the chief explained, was his bush soul; by killing the snake, the missionary would, in fact, be killing him. Without a trace of fear, the chief bent down, picked up the snake, and caressed it, apparently much to its liking. After asking the missionary not to say a word about the incident to anyone, he took the snake into another hut—to spare his guest's feelings—and lay down beside it.

This belief, known as nagualism, hangs on in Mexico and Central America to the present day, where the father of a newborn child will spread ashes outside the house to see which animal passes by first. Identified by the prints it leaves in the ash, that animal—whether bird, reptile, or mammal—then becomes the baby's so-called nagual, or guiding spirit. The child is taught that if he or she prays to the spirit, the nagual will come to his or her aid whenever it is needed. But since human and nagual are always linked, the death of one will bring about the death of the other.

In time, the veneration of animals by the earth's first inhabitants grew ever more complex. As primitive societies organized themselves into tribes and clans, the members identified themselves with particular animals, or totems, as did families within these groups. Unlike the nagual, bestowed on an individual more or less by fate or accident,

the totem sprang from an inherited system of belief. Clan members might revere the clan totem as an ancestor of their people or as their patron. To indicate their respect for the totem animal, the clan members sometimes took its name and in some cases they developed taboos against killing or eating the species.

In several groups, a young male was expected to have a totem of his own, much like a nagual, which he obtained through a prescribed rite that involved his going off alone into the wilderness and remaining there until an animal presented itself to him in a dream or a vision. Having thus acquired his own totem, he could expect the animal to confer a special magic on him. If the animal was a bear, it likely brought the assurance that the youth would come to no harm in bear country; if a beaver, that he would have no fear of water and hence would not drown. Sometimes he carried with him a medicine bundle that contained bits and pieces of his guardian animal—a bone, a feather, a bit of fur or hide—and that served as a kind of good luck charm. But for the protective magic of his totem to go on working for him, he generally had to worship the animal through various rituals and dances. Some individuals, of course, were more gifted in magic than others, and as they danced about mimicking their totems, a moment must have arrived when—falling into or reaching a trance—the dancers felt they were the animal.

Shapeshifting is the word most used to describe the metamorphosis of a man or woman into a beast. Literature and historical records are full of accounts of the phenomenon. Over the centuries, students of the subject have asked themselves a variety of questions: What actually happened during a shapeshifting experience? What forces came into play? What has made so many men and women from earliest times right up into the modern era willing to believe that a person could change shape? And what went on within the minds of those souls who were said to have undergone such a metamorphosis?

There are many theories, some founded in physical

To sneak up on bison, two Plains Indians resort to the immemorial disguise of animal skins—in this case, wolf hides. (When in a herd, bison apparently were not frightened by wolves.) The hunters may also have used the skins in hopes of assuming the wolf's powers.

science, some in psychology. If there is a neurological basis to lycanthropy, it may lie in the animal part of our brains, the so-called mammalian brain, a clump of neural tissue that sits at the top of the spine, wrapped in the convoluted mass of the cerebral cortex, the seat of human intelligence. We share this primitive core with other species as divergent as mouse and chimpanzee, our closest living relative on the evolutionary tree; it is the nub around which our cortical cells evolved. Some have postulated that it conceals primitive, atavistic powers that our ancestors knew how to tap and that we have since forgotten.

Certain psychoanalysts see the unconscious as being involved in the shapeshifting experience. Sigmund Freud envisioned the unconscious as a whole other realm in which the darkest secrets of the mind are kept, and his disciple Carl Jung spoke of a collective unconscious shared by all humans, a mutual repository as old as the species itself that contains remnants of our ancient lives in the form of archetypal images. Lycanthropy, some posit, gives vent to hidden impulses that spring from the unconscious or from the collective unconscious.

There can be no more vivid proof of the unconscious at work than dreams. We function under a veneer of daytime rationality, only to fall asleep at night and escape into a world where everything is possible. Here animals can take human form, humans can be animals. For primitive people, who put credence in their dreams, such metamorphoses remain proof of lycanthropy's power. Not long ago, an Amer-

A Festival to Please the Hunted

Almost totally dependent on such marine mammals as seals and walruses for sustenance, the Alaskan Inuit early saw a need to cultivate their living food sources. This concern led to the December Bladder Festival, in which they honor their prey.

Believing that an animal's bladder holds its soul, the Inuit preserve the organ after a successful hunt. At festival time, they inflate the collected bladders and decorate them with paint. Then, after cere-

monies that include ritual objects such as the caribou-human below, the Inuit carry the bladders to a hole in the ice, as shown in the ivory carving above.

There, they release the bladders into the water, anticipating that the souls within will rejoin their brethren beneath the ice and will reveal

how well they had been treated by the hunters. In fact, one shaman in the 1800s was lowered into the icy waters so that he could commune with the departing souls: He said that although some of the spirits complained of their treatment, others "were pleased with the men who had taken them and given them such a fine festival."

An Inuit Bladder ceremony carved on an ivory drill bow portrays the hunter at the center carrying inflated bladders on a pole.

With a human face but a deer's body, this caribou effigy, a ritual object used in the Bladder Festival, exemplifies the Inuit belief in the kinship between humans and animals. The Inuit hold that an animal's soul can not only show itself, but also speak.

Feathered masks such as this are worn in the Inuit Bladder ceremony. They represent the spirits of the animals, as well as of the wearers, and are intended for the symbolic enjoyment of the Inuit's prey.

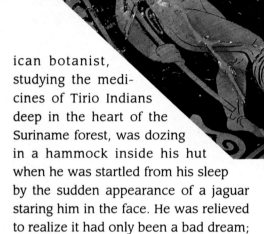

An ecstatic maenad, a votary of the fertility god Dionysus, cavorts with a dismembered leg on a Greek vase. In early rites, maenads ate human flesh.

ican botanist, studying the medicines of Tirio Indians deep in the heart of the Suriname forest, was dozing in a hammock inside his hut when he was startled from his sleep by the sudden appearance of a jaguar staring him in the face. He was relieved to realize it had only been a bad dream; but when he told his nightmare to the local sorcerer or shaman, whom he had befriended in hopes of learning the "magic" of certain plants, the Indian merely smiled and said, "That was me."

Shapeshifting crops up commonly in our legends and myths, those public, wish-fulfillment dreams of ancient peoples. The Greek god Zeus transformed himself regularly, thinking nothing of becoming a dove, a bull, a swan, a ram, a snake, or an eagle, if it meant that he might more easily seduce a comely goddess or winsome mortal.

From such unions sprang Zeus's many progeny, among them the god Dionysus. According to one legend, Zeus became a serpent in order to seduce Persephone, who then gave birth to Dionysus. Entering the world with a horn on his head, the child immediately climbed up onto his father's throne and began wielding Zeus's thunderbolts. (In another version of the myth, Dionysus is described as "the last king of the gods appointed by Zeus," who "set him on the kingly throne, and placed in his hand the scepter, and made him king of all the gods of the world.") As he stood admiring himself in a mirror, the precocious babe was attacked by Titans, who began stabbing him with their knives. Being very much his father's son, Dionysus resorted to shapeshifting to escape his attackers: He took on the image first of Zeus and then of Cronus, Zeus's enemy, and when the Titans did not let up, he turned himself successively into

a youth, a lion, a horse, and a snake, before finally metamorphosing into a bull. And in that form, he was cut to bits by the Titans.

The story of Dionysus has several different endings. In one version, the slaughtered victim is pieced together by his mother and brought back to life; in several other endings, he rises from the dead soon after his burial and ascends into heaven.

The myth of Dionysus inspired an early dramatic example of psychological shapeshifting by mortals who took on the behavioral characteristics of animals. Women called maenads, priestesses of the Dionysian cult, would dance madly about the countryside, representing spirits of the dead and suckling wolf pups and the young of other beasts at their breasts. Dressed in wildcat or lynx skins and probably intoxicated by consuming Asian ivy, a plant with psychoactive effects, these frenetic women would descend on a sacrificial bull. Regarding it as the living representative of Dionysus, god of agriculture, as well the patron of trees and grapevines, they would proceed to tear the unfortunate animal to pieces with their bare hands and their teeth, drink its blood, and eat its still quivering flesh.

By killing the bull, the maenads were reenacting Dionysus's passion, and by drinking the blood of the animal and eating its flesh, they were incorporating the god into themselves, signifying his resurrection. The bloody sacrifice seems to have been designed to assure the farmers that life would go on, just as it had for Dionysus himself, and

Transformed into a swan, the powerful and lascivious Greek god Zeus approaches the human princess Leda, as depicted in this German tapestry. Out of their union was born the beautiful Helen of Troy, who was hatched, according to ancient mythology, from a swan's egg.

that grape vines, trees, and the land itself would all continue to bear fruit.

Far to the north, in the darker lands of Scandinavia, another group of mortals underwent a similar psychological transformation with equal animal ferocity. They were the berserkers, a special breed of Viking warriors who were as fierce and maniacal as the maenads were. But the sole purpose of the berserkers was to vanquish and kill their enemies, not to encourage life. The men had as their patron Odin, god of death, who was just as handy at shapeshifting as Zeus himself was.

Throwing off their human identity, the berserkers took on the fierce qualities of bears or wolves, and went growling and yelping into battle. Clothed only in the animals' skins, with their eyes glaring "as though a flame burned in their sockets," they mimicked in their brutality the creatures' savagery. They believed themselves invulnerable to sword or fire. So fiercely and irrationally did the berserkers behave and so superhuman was their strength that some historians think they were acting under the influence of a drug, perhaps fly agaric, a hallucinogenic mushroom. This seems borne out by the fact that during battle they foamed at the mouth and bit the edges of their shields like rabid dogs.

While some berserkers were organized as fighting units and followed a warlord, others roamed the countryside in lawless bands, lusting for booty. In particular, they took advantage of a then current Norwegian law that declared that any man who declined an invitation to single combat would forfeit all his estate, his wife, and his children to the challenger. The berserkers simply matched their most formidable member with a meek farmer, and the spoils were theirs with no hand raised.

If a drug accounts for their fierceness, its effect was apparently permanently mind-altering, as attested in the sagas, prose narratives set down in the twelfth and thirteenth centuries in Iceland, celebrating the heroic deeds of Icelanders and the Norwegians from whom the Icelanders descended. One tells of Thorir, who was overcome by berserk-

er fits, "a sad misfortune to such a man, as they were quite beyond control." One medieval saga describes the lifetime affliction of a man named Ulf, meaning "the wolf": "Ulf was so tall and strong that the like of him was not to be seen in the land at that time. And when he was young, he was on Viking expeditions and harrying." Ulf was a landed squire and "a good advisor, he was so clear headed." But "every day, when it grew towards dusk, he became so savage that few dared exchange a word with him. People said that he was much given to *hamrammr* (changing form), so he was called Kveldulf, the evening wolf." With the arrival of morn-

In a design for a Viking helmet plate, a wolf-like creature, thought to be a berserker, dances with a youth. The berserkers, noted for their fierceness, got their name from the bear skins some wore, although wolf hides were also used.

upon the quarter deck, he raised his cleaver, and smote Hallvard through the helm and head, so that the haft was buried in the flesh; but he dragged it to him so violently that he whisked Hallvard into the air, and flung him overboard." The few raiders who survived the onslaught of Kveldulf's group jumped into the sea, but the berserkers rowed after them, killing all they could find, "and thus perished Hallvard with fifty men."

With the spread of Christianity throughout pagan Europe, shapeshifting, whether genuine or imaginary, came under the religion's attack. The Church despised the notion of transformation, considering it the work of the devil. "No one must let himself think that a man can really be transformed into an animal, or an animal into a man," wrote one theologian. "These are magical portents and illusions, having the form but not the substance of those things which they present to our sight."

Despite such attacks on its credibility, the belief in shapeshifting survived. Superstition offered it fertile ground, and like some pale forest mushroom, it continued to proliferate for centuries in the shadowed crannies and outreaches of Europe. Church records down through the decades are filled with accounts of attempts by the pope and his missionaries to curtail the practice. In the eleventh century, the pope admonished the Danish king not only because there were still too many sorcerers worshiping pagan gods in an ostensibly Christian land but also because they had a reputation, whether deserved or not, for being able to turn themselves into cats and wolves.

People believed that in order to be transformed the shapeshifter had to do little more than rub his or her body with special ointment or salve, wear a belt or girdle made from the skin of the animal that individual wanted to become, consume some of the creature's brains, drink water from its footprint, or recite an incantation or cast a spell. Although the metamorphosis was generally seen as a voluntary act, it could also be triggered as a punishment, inflicted on an unsuspecting individual by a malevolent soul. According to some, the phenomenon was even contagious;

ing, he would be found in bed, totally worn out by his night-time peregrinations.

The *Aigla Saga* throws additional light on the popular ideas about berserker savagery. One summer day, Kveldulf and his son, Skallagrim, caught sight of a ship approaching their port. Assembling two boats and forty men, they rowed out to the alien vessel and boarded it, whereupon a berserker frenzy overtook Kveldulf and many of his band. As the saga notes, "They slew all the men who were before them." But the leader of the piratical expedition, a man called Hallvard, had yet to fall. "Now when Kveldulf came brushing up against the shapeshifter's clothing or eating his food would be enough to damn an unwary innocent to a life of shapeshifting.

Among the most avid shapeshifters in Europe were, of course, witches, and the literature of lycanthropy is filled with stories of their deeds. Witchery was considered to be a glamorous profession—that is, if glamour can be taken in its original meaning, namely, the ability to create illusions, to fool ordinary people into believing that things are other than they seem. Confessions of witches and the testimony of their accusers offer insights into the mechanics of their alleged glamour and into the workings of lycanthropy itself. Indeed, to understand how witches acquired their reputation for turning themselves into animals, it is first necessary to understand something about their oft noted talent for flying.

To be transported out of this world, the witches were said to use potent magic, salves which they applied to various parts of their bodies, as well as to their broomsticks. According to popular accounts, the components of these varied, from tansy, hellebore, and wild ginger mixed with egg and fried in butter, to "fat of children, wild celery juice, clinging birthwort, tormentilla, nightshade and soot." The English philosopher and essayist Francis Bacon, while noting that witches' salves were commonly believed to be "made of the fat of children digged out of their graves," gave more credence to their use of such ingredients as the "soperiferous medicines," namely "henbane, hemlock, mandrake, moonshade, tobacco, opium, saffron, poplar leaves, etc." The authors of a German interrogation manual of 1558, which was used to help wring information from accused witches, did not doubt the necessity for human fat in the salves. To their knowledge, they claimed, it was rendered "by boiling or frying."

Whatever their components, the salves had some powerful effects. One old hag let a Dominican friar observe her undergo a spell. She crawled into a baking trough, rubbed herself well with salve, and fell asleep. "Then she imagined that she was flying," recounted the source, "and she had all her pleasures internally. She fought with her hands and feet, and did that so violently that the trough fell off the bench and she came to lie under it, gashing her head." Another observer reported how he and some colleagues watched a witch undress, anoint herself with salve, and fall on the floor "profoundly asleep," whereupon the men "not very gently tanned her hide." Not only did she not waken; she did not feel the blows. Eventually, she came around and "told many strange tales about how she travelled over dale and mountain. We disputed it and pointed to the wheals on her body, but that was for naught. In short, all our remonstrances and actions amounted to no more than if somebody blew into a cold stove."

Now, if witches did not actually fly (and the question was much debated, even by so prominent a figure as Martin Luther), the psychic effects of their ointments were enough to convince them that they had indeed traveled hither and yon during their trances. And it was easy for people to imagine that witches' souls, loosed from their constraints by the salves' effects, could enter other creatures. Even those doubters who put no credence in witches' flying often credited them with the ability to escape the prisons of their bodies and transform themselves into cats, hares, mice, ravens, and bees.

The thought of a witch's malign spirit inside a small animal—one that because of its size could easily slip into a house and do evil—terrified people. Old records abound with stories of witches disguised as cats that were apprehended or wounded just as they were about to carry out their evil intent. Either the cat reverted instantly to witch, or the witch would turn up later bearing a cut exactly where the cat had received its wound, a phenomenon that students of transformation call wound doubling. (Wound doubling appears worldwide in the annals of witchcraft and is echoed in the stories of the young English lieutenant beset by hyenas in Africa.)

Among the voluminous transcriptions of witches' trials in England is one account describing how an old woman

Bringing Beastly Criminals to Justice

Trying a sow for murder and then executing her may sound improbable, but it happened—more than once, in fact, in the days when belief in transformation and spirit possession was common. Indeed, in medieval Europe at least thirty-four pigs were convicted of murdering children and duly punished, as in the scene at right, in which a sow, found guilty of maiming and killing a child by a French court in 1386, is about to be hanged.

The charges were usually based on actual incidents; the pig might very well have bitten or trampled an infant to death, say. But to try the pig, rather than the parent who left the baby in an unsafe place or the farmer whose sow strayed into a human dwelling, was in the old tradition of punishing scape-animals (in biblical times, usually scapegoats) for human sins.

Nor were pigs the only offenders brought to justice by Europeans: Locusts, flies, caterpillars, slugs, termites, mice, rats, moles, dogs, bulls, and goats, among others, were tried by civic or ecclesiastical courts. Between the years 824 and 1845, no fewer than 144 prosecutions led to the execution or excommunication of a variety of creatures said to have been possessed by demons or the devil himself.

Sometimes a group of pests, such as a swarm of locusts, was tried in absentia. In a case involving insects that were laying waste to grapevines around the French city of Troyes in 1516, not only was a prosecutor heard on behalf of the vineyard owners, but counsel was assigned to represent the accused. The bugs were threatened with anathema—a Church ban or curse —if they did not leave within a week. What happened at the end of the seven days, alas, went unrecorded, but in a similar case, in which termites were accused of undermining a monastery, the threat allegedly worked, with the insects abandoning the woodwork and filing out of the building in columns.

In judicial proceedings, witnesses would be called, and the lawyers for the defense and prosecution would present their arguments with all the vigor they would have given to the trial of a human murderer. Sentences proceeded according to the letter of the law. In the case of a porcine killer, as a 1403 bill for goods and services indicates, the sow was jailed and conveyed in a carriage to the scaffold; the so-called master of high works was brought from Paris to carry out the execution, and new gloves were purchased for him so that the man would not have to dirty his hands when he hanged the condemned porker.

These trials served to remind people that evil lay everywhere and must be routed out or somehow understood if the natural laws governing the universe were not to be undermined by the extraordinary behavior of animals and insects. As one modern student of such zealotry has put it, "the job of the courts was to domesticate chaos"—to help make sense out of something as apparently senseless as a pig taking the life of an innocent child.

called Julian Cox was apprehended in the year 1663 and indicted for having transformed herself into a hare. The record states: "The first witness was a huntsman, who swore that he went out with a pack of hounds to hunt a hare, and not far from her house, he at last started a hare. The dogs hunted her very close, and the third ring hunted her in view, till at last the huntsman perceiving the hare almost spent, and making toward a great bush he ran on the other side of the bush to take her up, and preserve her from the dogs. But as soon as he laid hands on her, it proved to be Julian Cox, who had her head grovelling on the ground and her globes (as he expressed it) upward. He knowing her, was so affrighted that his hair on his head stood on end, and yet he spake to her and asked her what brought her there; but she was so far out of breath, that she could not make him any answer. His dogs also came up with full cry to recover the game and smelt at her, and so left off hunting any farther. And the huntsman went home presently, sadly affrighted."

A court record from a trial conducted in 1719 gives colorful evidence of the wound doubling of animal and witch so often cited as evidence of a witch's maleficence and link to the devil. One William Montgomery came home to find his house invaded by cats "speaking among themselves," the document states matter-of-factly. They belonged to no one in the neighborhood, and since Montgomery's frightened wife and maidservant wanted him to get rid of them, he began driving them away. One cat got in a chest and thrust out her neck through a hole in its side. Montgomery fastened his sword on her neck, "which cut her" but did not kill her, nor, curiously, did it cause her to bleed. "Having (at length) opened the chest, my servant fixed my dirk [a long, flat-sided dagger] in her hinder quarter, which continued there till I thought, by many strokes, I had killed her with my sword; and having cast her out dead, she could not be found the next morning."

Several nights later, the cats returned and once again Montgomery fought with them. He managed to trap one of the creatures in a piece of plaid, thrust his dirk through her body, "and having fixed the dirk in the ground, I drove at her head with the back of an axe until she was dead, and being cast out could not be found next morning." And again there was no blood.

Not long afterward, two women in the neighborhood died suddenly of unknown causes, and something most unusual happened to a woman by the name of Margaret Nin-Gilbert, whose house was only a half a mile or so away from Montgomery's. As she dragged herself to her door one day, one of her legs fell off! Having long suspected her of being a witch, the neighbors who witnessed this bizarre happening picked up the swollen and blackened limb and carried it to the sheriff, who promptly arrested Margaret Nin-Gilbert on a charge of witchcraft. In the confession that was wrung out of her, she admitted that she had been among the witches in cat disguise at Montgomery's house and said that either his axe or dirk had broken her leg, which then putrefied and dropped off. And among her companions at his place, she stated, had been the two women who had just died.

So prevalent were witches in metamorphosed form—or at least that is what much of the general public believed—that some people spotted them around every corner; one sixteenth-century gentleman did not dare even go out into his garden. "I am afraid," he admitted, "for I see now and then a hare, which my conscience giveth me is a witch, or some witch's spirit, she stareth so upon me. And sometimes I see an ugly weasel run through my yard, and there is a foul cat sometimes in my barn, which I have no liking unto." Some animals were even put on trial and duly punished for their alleged crimes (page 40).

A few individuals found themselves sufficiently appalled by the punishments handed out to convicted witches by corrupt or overzealous officials to think twice about whether the accused were witches at all or simply maligned victims of other people's paranoia. One official had seen hundreds of burnings at the stake and tortures so gruesome that he would gladly pay a fortune, he said, if only he could forget them.

The Tibetan priests in this 1906 painting wear oversize masks in order to take on the roles of old animal-gods from the pre-Buddhist Bon religion. Their processional dance is probably intended to drive away evil spirits.

His anger whelmed up in a bold statement: "Listen you money-hungering judges and bloodthirsty prosecutors, the apparitions of the Devil are all lies. It is high time the rulers appointed better judges and put faith in more moderate preachers, and then the Devil with his deceiving illusions would be put to shame."

Shapeshifting was a belief as deeply rooted in the rest of the world as it was in Europe. The folklore of India, China, and Japan, among other countries, as well as that of the Indians of the Americas, is rich in tales of transformations. There exists a kind of universal protagonist of many of these tales, an animal that transforms itself into a human or possesses humanlike qualities, that enjoys outwitting people and often takes advantage of them sexually. Students of this genre of legend have labeled this character, whether it appears as a fox or a *tanuki* in Japan or as a coyote in the American Southwest, as the trickster. There is a good deal of humor in trickster stories *(pages 49-55)*, but these shapeshifters were also often seen as purveyors of evil, and many were re-

vealed through the same kind of wound doubling that caused poor Margaret Nin-Gilbert's downfall.

In China, for example, it was told how during the first month of 1755, babies in what is now Beijing were dying of convulsions during the early hours of the morning. Wherever they struggled for life, an owl was observed flying into the death chamber. Hearing of the owl, an archer went to a room where an infant was dying and waited for the owl to enter. The moment it fluttered into view, he shot one of his arrows at the bird. Crying out in pain, the owl escaped, leaving a trail of blood that led to the kitchen of a military man. And there the archer discovered a servant woman with green eyes, incapacitated by a wound in her loin. Needless to say, the wound was enough to establish her connection to the bird and bring about her confession. She admitted leaving her abode at midnight, in the guise of an owl, so that she might feed on the brains of babies. As in the case of her European sisters, the woman was burned alive, and with her body reduced to ashes, the epidemic of convulsions allegedly came to an end.

The Navajo of the American Southwest also regard shapeshifters as evil beings. They see them as misusing their power in order to engage in incest, to hurt or otherwise harm individuals, and to steal from the dead. Acting out of self-protection, the Navajo have been known to track down and kill those members of the tribe who they believe are lycanthropes.

Navajo shapeshifting lore centers on witches, male as well as female, and in many ways parallels eerily the witchcraft lore of Europe. While dressed in the skins of such fierce animals as the coyote, wolf, and bear, whose qualities they naturally assume, the witches are said to roam about at night, ready to drop a noxious powder through the smoke hole of a hogan or directly into the nostrils or mouths of their victims.

This dusty substance, which resembles pollen, is prepared by grinding the flesh and bones of the dead, especially those of children—and is considered all the more effective for being made from the remains of twins. Particularly prized are the bones at the back of the neck and the skin of fingertips, with its characteristic pattern of whorls. When administered through any of the sinister means described above, or simply blown into the face of the intended target, or slipped into a cigarette, the preparation is believed to induce a variety of conditions, ranging from lockjaw and a black and swollen tongue, to unconsciousness. Sometimes the effects are not immediate, however, and the victim might be left to just slowly fade away.

The Navajo claim they can tell when a witch is close by. His or her presence is signaled by the sudden barking of dogs at night; a trickle of dirt descending into a hogan from the smoke hole, dislodged by the alien on the roof; or odd, unexplained noises outside. Invariably the transformed witch leaves tracks, and generally these prints are bigger than the tracks of the actual animal whose skin the interloper wears. When the trail is followed, it often leads to the home of a tribe member previously unsuspected of practicing the black arts.

Hopi Indians, neighbors of the Navajo, take a kindlier view of shapeshifters. They feel there is no essential difference between humans and other forms of life. Only outward appearances separate the species from one another; and when the external is penetrated, their commonality emerges. The Hopi preserve their connection to the gods or nature spirits, and like the earliest of humans, they consider themselves one with the earth and all its wonders. They find peace and stability through the cooperation and hard work their harsh desert environment continually demands of them. Believing in shapeshifting, they regard it as yet another manifestation of the close bond between the earth and the gods and see it as a power that, though given to certain individuals, belongs to the group as a whole and can be used for the good of all.

In Africa, too, lycanthropy has been slow to die. As late as the 1950s, initiates of the Isawiyya brotherhood of Morocco would wear animal masks at meetings and imitate the behavior of animals represented by their headgear—lions, panthers, wildcats, boars, jackals, dogs, and camels. They would be carefully scrutinized by the elders and, according to how well they mimicked the creatures, they would then be given secret names for those they most resembled in temperament and behavior.

As full-fledged members of the brotherhood, they joined packs or herds, and once a year the packs would go about masquerading as wild beasts. With their hands and feet dyed with henna to give them a blood-stained appearance, the participants made the rounds of their neighborhoods, demanding live animals from villagers and farmers. Those brethren designated as lions, panthers, jackals, cats, and dogs had the unenviable duty of tearing to pieces with their teeth the live goats, sheep, and oxen that they were given. Families were obliged to donate one sacrificial animal each. Any reluctant to do so were roundly cursed for their refusal and often found their flocks or herds raided at night, ostensibly by jackals.

Horrific though this maenadlike ritual may have been, it pales besides an Isawiyya rite witnessed by a German writer in the second half of the nineteenth century. Describing how the cult's initiates threw themselves into a frenzy during a dance, the author provides a rare glimpse into the lycanthropic excesses of the past. "The movements become more and more rapid," he writes, "the bending deeper and deeper, the turnings of the head and the body more and more violent, until at length the exhausted Isawiyya are seized with vertigo, froth gathers on their lips, their eyes stand out of their sockets and roll with the shifting gaze of the insane, and the fanatical dancers fall staggering to the ground; they have attained blissful ecstacy."

"Soon they are wallowing in wild disorder, giving vent to frightful yells of an altogether unhuman character, and resembling now the snorting of the wild boar, now the roaring of the lion. Some of them, like wild beasts, grind their teeth, from which drips a whitish foam. In their disordered and threatening movements, it would seem as if they are about to rend the onlookers in pieces."

The Isawiyya were now ready to receive the spirit of the founder of the brotherhood, which, according to their belief, would make them immune to poison and to "all things that lacerate and cut." To prove that the moment was at hand, a large dish containing scorpions, toads, serpents, lizards—"a jumble of loathsome and venomous creatures"—was brought forward and emptied out onto the ground. Without hesitation, the men pounced "upon the foul mass of living things with the voracity of famished beasts of prey, and in a moment the whole is torn in pieces and devoured. No trickery here! I see the reptiles torn in pieces by the powerful teeth, while the blood of the serpents and the slimy secretion of the scorpions tinge the saliva at the corners of the mouth."

As unpleasant as such a ritual may appear to the uninitiated, it cannot begin to match the repellent character of the lycanthropic crimes of the so-called leopard-men of Africa. This predacious group survived well into the twentieth century, despite legal efforts to bring the bloodthirsty ways of the leopard-men to a halt. They shared an identification with the leopard as a stealthy predator and mimicked its ruthlessness as a killer. The men dressed according to the role, wearing leopard skins or a spotted garment; sometimes they covered their bodies with makeup and their faces with masks or veils. On their feet the leopard-men frequently donned sandals or shoes whose soles they had incised with the shapes of the cat's paws, so that the shoes would leave paw prints around the corpse. Most sinister of all were their instruments of death—long, clawlike knives that they carried either in their hands or attached to their fingers or to gloves.

Fundamental to their success, they believed, was a medicine bundle, or fetish, called *borfimah*. The contents of the bag might include parts of the cadaver of a first-born female child, fat from the kidneys of a human sacrifice, skin from the sole and palm of the victim, pieces of genitals and liver, and blood. Whatever its components, the borfimah supposedly offered protection to the leopard-men on their murderous forays.

Thus emboldened, the killers would pounce upon their human prey and sever the carotid artery in the victim's neck. "They hide in the bush until dusk," relates one author, writing in 1891. "If any person should pass, the leopard men spring upon him or her as the case may be, and kill them on the spot. The leopard men then mutilate the body in a dreadful manner, taking away certain portions and leaving the horrible spectacle on the roadside. It is said that the parts which they take away the leopard men eat. The last body found was that of a man. The head had been opened and the brains taken out, the right hand and left foot cut off, and the heart also taken away."

Among more recent accounts of the leopard-men, a police report dating from 1946 confirms these grisly details, while adding a few of its own to the record: "In all parts of the area the killings seemed to conform to the same rough, general pattern. The victims were generally waylaid in the evening on a bush path on their way back from market or farm, or in the bush whilst gathering edible leaves, killed by stabbing or clubbing and their bodies mutilated in a characteristic fashion, partly, it is thought, for purposes of ritual, and partly to simulate the injuries caused by a wild animal.

45

Typical mutilations consist of decapitation and denuding the skull from all flesh, severing of one of the arms and removing the tissues from it, the removing and scraping of the cervical vertebrae, and the removal of the heart and lungs which are always taken away by the murderers. Often all these mutilations are found on one body but at other times only some are present. In some cases there are no mutilations apart from stab wounds usually in the neck, which appear to have been made by sharp iron spikes used locally for cooking yams. It is a characteristic feature of the leopard killings that the victim is more often than not accompanied by other people at the time he is attacked—the leopard murderer does not appear to mind being seen by witnesses in the act of killing, confident as he is that his charm will protect him and that he will be able to intimidate the

A gruesome instrument of murder, the iron claw of an African leopard-man (right) is shown with a paw-print stamp (above), used to make it look like a big cat was the killer. The claw was employed to sever the carotid artery, then tear out the victim's insides.

witnesses into keeping silent.''

Although rumors of cannibalism often cropped up in written reports of leopard-men, the allegation is difficult to substantiate, in part because so many of the murderers belonged to secret societies, about which neither the members nor frightened outsiders were prepared to talk. It was often said that initiates were given human flesh to eat without their knowing it and that once they consumed such meat, there could be no turning back for them; they were well on their way to becoming murderers themselves—a developmental pattern similar to that ascribed to werewolves and vampires in European tradition.

No completely satisfactory theory has ever been put forth to explain what drove the leopard-men to such bestiality or why they were so willing to believe themselves to be cats. Some would blame it on psychic influences alone, others on a witch doctor's medicine, which may well have included a potent drug of some kind. The words of a thirty-seven-year-old American anthropologist, who turned into a tiger, or at least thought he did, may shed light on the intensity of the leopard-men's belief and on the phenomenon of lycanthropy in general. They are recorded in a book, *The Varieties of Psychedelic Experience,* a collection of anonymous subjects' reactions to psychochemicals, compiled by R. E. L. Masters and Jean Houston.

Long fascinated by the notion of transformations, the anthropologist made himself the subject of an experiment that carried a large measure of risk for him. Indeed, it was much more perilous, probably, than he or many others could have realized in that era, the 1960s, when the dangers of permanent damage from psychedelic drugs were not widely recognized. Alone in his apartment, he took 500 micrograms of LSD. With pencil and paper at his side, he lay down and gave himself over to the drug and some ritualistic music that he had put on his record player. Later he was able to reconstruct from his notes the metamorphosis he underwent, as sinister in its way as Robert Louis Stevenson's famous description of Dr. Jekyll turning into Mr. Hyde: ''The first phase of my experience was on a human level. As I managed to scribble, before again abandoning myself (appropriate term!) to the recording, this was my first authentic experience of the orgiastic. I was totally *there,* totally a participant, and what I participated in was a frenzied dionysiac union with a multiplicity of others: the forging of single will or emotional state, I cannot say which, but perhaps a will to yield utterly to a wild, animalistic sensuality and emotional outpouring—an ecstasy in which particular bodies were abandoned for a single body constituted of us all, a body writhing as if in the throes of an almost unbearable onslaught of sensuality."

Then, after the passage of perhaps twenty minutes, the anthropologist became conscious of himself "moving across the floor of the apartment, moving as best I can recall by propelling myself along on my knees with my flattened palms also pressed against the floor. At about the same instant I found myself before a full-length mirror and, looking into it, was confronted by a huge, magnificent specimen of a tiger! Simultaneous, I think, with my perception of this image I became aware of my tiger's body, of emotions that seemed to saturate my being, and of a narrow or compressed kind of consciousness that focused only upon what was being perceived and upon the emotional state on the one hand and basic physical sensation on the

When wearing a garment like this, a leopard-man concealed his human features beneath the hood. By identifying with the spotted predator, he felt empowered to kill with as much ruthlessness as the beast itself.

other. I was *in* this body, and *felt* this body, as I never have been in or felt my own.

"Confronting the image in the mirror, I knew and yet did not know that this image was my own (although, oddly, it seemed to me later that there was, in the face of this tiger, something of my face). I reacted to the image, partly anyhow, as if it might be another tiger with whom I had come unexpectedly face to face. Yet something in me questioned the reality of the image, and I recall my bafflement when I ran my claws across the glass and touched the hard, flat surface. All the while I was making spitting and snarling noises and my muscles were tensed in readiness for combat. Finally, I turned away from the mirror and padded restlessly around the apartment, still making those sounds that somehow indicated to me bafflement and rage."

Next the anthropologist-cum-tiger found himself "locked up in a cage in some zoo. It seems that I paced interminably up and down within the barred enclosure, looking out with a kind of flattened vision at people like paper cutouts who stood peering into my cage."

As he began to drift back to reality, the anthropologist felt regret over leaving the powerful transformation behind him. Although he had not been very happy as a tiger, he recognized that "the tiger represented some valid and essential aspect of what or who I am."

When at last he had returned to his normal state of mind, the man asked himself whether he would have resembled in any way a tiger to someone observing him during the most intense part of his psychedelic experience. "Somehow I think the answer to that is 'Yes,'" he wrote. He knew, of course, from his readings that a shapeshifter believes himself or herself transformed and that the spectator is often convinced that the shapeshifter has indeed taken on certain animal qualities. But then reason overtook him once more and he was reduced to wondering whether "I could only have looked like a silly anthropologist, 'out of his skull' on hallucinogens, foolishly crawling around on the floor and making a lot of noises."

But, in fact, would he have thus appeared? One of the eeriest accounts in the literature of lycanthropy describes the experience of a Mr. K, an Englishman, who early in this century witnessed something quite amazing in the shadowy depths of the Indian jungle. "Anxious to see if there was anything of truth in the alleged materialization of the tiger totem to those supplicating it," he related to a friend, "I went one evening to a spot in the jungle—some two or three miles from the village—where I had been informed the manifestations took place." He arrived at "a circular clearing of about twenty feet in diameter, surrounded on all sides by rank grass of a prodigious height." Hidden by the vegetation, he waited there for the appearance of the tiger-man, who, to his surprise, turned out to be "hardly more than a boy—slim and almost feminine." The youth had come "gallivanting along the narrow path through the brushwood, like some careless, brown-skinned hoyden." But the moment he reached the circle, his demeanor changed; he became humble and respectful.

As Mr. K peeked through the grass, the boy knelt down "and, touching the ground three times in succession with his forehead, looked up at the giant kulpa-tree opposite him, chanting as he did so some weird and monotonous refrain." Although the sky had been ablaze with stars and moonlight, it now darkened, as "an unnatural, awe-inspiring shade seemed to swoop down from the far distant mountains and to hush into breathless silence everything it touched." The Englishman was deeply affected: "I had not believed in the supernatural, and now I was confronted with a dread of what I could not understand and could not analyse—of something that suggested an appearance, alarming on account of its very vagueness."

His pulse quickened and became irregular, and he grew faint and sick, "painfully susceptible to a sensation of excessive coldness, which instinct told me was quite independent of any actual change in the atmosphere."

Suddenly, out of the jungle came "a cry, half human and half animal." Soon footsteps could be heard; they were "the footsteps of something running towards us and covering the ground with huge, light strides. Nearer and nearer it came, till, with a sudden spring, it burst into view—the giant reeds were dashed aside, and I saw standing in front of the kulpa-tree a vertical column of crimson light of perhaps seven feet in height and one or so in width. A column—only a column, though the

suggestion conveyed to me by the column was nasty—nasty with a nastiness that baffles description."

The boy reacted with fear. "For some seconds he only gasped; then, by degrees, the rolling of his eyes and the twitching of his lips ceased. He stretched out a hand and made some sign on the ground. Then he produced a string of beads, and after placing it over the scratchings he had made on the soil, jerked out some strange incantation in a voice that thickened and quivered with terror. I then saw a stream of red light steal from the base of the column and dart like forked lightning to the beads, which instantly shone a luminous red."

Picking up the beads, the boy put them around his neck, clapped his hands together, and let out a succession of high-pitched cries "that gradually became more and more animal in tone, and finally ended in a roar." The darkness that had fallen over the spot yielded to moonlight, and in that brightness Mr. K saw, "peering up at me, the yellow, glittering, malevolent eyes, not of a man, but a tiger—a tiger thirsting for human blood."

Paralyzed by the transformation that he had beheld, the man was unable at first to move. Then he began to run, chased by the beast he had seen. He reached the safety of a tree and scrambled up into its branches just as "a long hairy paw, with black, gleaming claws shot past my cheek." He had given himself up for lost, when, to his amazement, the creature "gave a growl of terror and, bounding away, was speedily lost in the jungle."

The next morning the half-eaten bodies of a father, mother, and son were found on the floor of their hut. From the evidence, it was plain that a tiger had attacked and killed them. But as Mr. K subsequently discovered, the dead were known to all as the sworn enemies of the young man he had seen cowering before the column of crimson light. Rational people would consider this coincidence. Perhaps Mr. K was still under the influence of his experience when he apparently judged the tiger's choice of victims to be other than mere chance. "It was not," he said, "difficult to guess at the identity of their destroyer."

Tricks of the Shapeshifters

The archetypal shapeshifter, the transformer to whom all matter is malleable, is the trickster, world builder and hero of the earliest stories in a variety of cultures. The many myths about tricksters show them to be clever but gullible, amoral and mischievous, sometimes evil. Though represented as a familiar animal—as the raven or coyote of Native American tales, for example—a trickster personifies a primitive side of human nature, an early stage in human awareness when little distinction was made between people and the world around them.

That world was said in many myths to be the creation of a trickster. One such creator is Raven, hero of a cycle of tales told by the Tlingit tribes of the American Northwest. Raven provided the very earth for humanity to live on, and in the tale retold on pages 50 and 51, he then added stars, moon, and sun to the sky; but like other tricksters, he never meant to be of service, he only wanted to relieve his own boredom.

Indeed, selfishness is a cardinal trait of tricksters. Unable to see past their own desires, they have little self-control and no regard for consequences—which can be dire indeed. Human mortality itself is blamed on a trickster in many tales, including one told by the Nez Percé Indians of Idaho and Montana that begins on page 52. A trickster may also bring disaster to himself, especially if he is imprudent in making enemies. Japanese tricksters can be particularly malicious, and some of their pranks *(pages 54 and 55)* invite a gruesome revenge.

A Greedy Grandson's Cosmic Theft

In Tlingit tribal legends of the American Northwest, the greatest trickster is Raven, a shape-shifter and creator. He was born magically after his mother, a princess in the Land of Supernatural Beings, swallowed a pebble. But he eventually angered his uncle, a mighty chief. Needing to escape the floods his uncle sent to kill him, Raven created the earth, so the tales say, from a handful of sand. In his creating, however, Raven forgot to make light. Soon, bored with his world's darkness, he resolved to steal the sun away from the Sky Chief, who kept it in a box hung from the ceiling of his heavily guarded house.

Raven flew to the Sky World but could not get into the house. The Sky Chief, however, had a daughter, so Raven became a hemlock needle and fell into her drinking water. The maiden swallowed him and became pregnant, and soon Raven was reborn as the great chief's grandson.

The chief could deny his grandson nothing. When the child squalled for the precious boxes hung from the ceiling, the old man gave him one as a toy. Left alone with the box, young Raven opened it to find no sun but only stars. Disappointed, the boy played for a time with the bright baubles, then flung them out through the roof's smoke hole. The stars scattered to the celestial places they hold to this day. Starlight, however, was too faint for Raven, and he begged for another treasure box. Again

the old man gave in, and again the boy opened the box. This time he found the moon and tossed it out of the smoke hole and into its place in the sky.

Knowing the last box held the sun, Raven renewed his piteous cries and the Sky Chief took down the box. Instantly Raven resumed his bird shape and flew with the box out of the smoke hole and far away, alighting on the earth. Then he took a man's shape, picked up the box, and walked north, until he came to an impassable river. He saw people on the far shore, but when he asked them to help him cross, they refused. Even when he told them he was bringing the bright light of day, they would not help. Exasperated, Raven opened the box and released the brilliant, blinding light.

Dazzled and frightened by the light, the people fled. Those who happened to be wearing furs and hides plunged into the woods to become Forest People, the animals who live there still. The villagers who were garbed in the hides of sea animals dived into the water, becoming Sea People—sea lions, seals, fishes, and whales. And those clothed in bird skins took flight, becoming the winged People of the Sky.

According to Tlingit tradition, this story shows how the beasts, birds, and fishes came to be and proves that they are but humans in disguise. All of these creatures resume their true human form when they are alone—or when the occasion demands it.

When Coyote Lost Humanity's Immortality

Before the human race appeared on the earth, so the Nez Percé legends say, Coyote lived happily with his wife. But the woman died before him, and he was very lonely. The death spirit, pale and indistinct, came to Coyote and offered to take him to his wife. "But," the spirit warned, "you must do everything exactly as I say." Coyote agreed, and they set off.

As they went, Coyote did all that the ghost did, repeating the words the phantom spoke and imitating his movements. At last the spirit told Coyote that they had come to a very long lodge and that his wife was inside. The ghost lifted the door flap and entered, and Coyote did the same, although he saw only the open prairie.

Then the spirit explained, "You will see that things here are different; when darkness falls in the land of the living, dawn comes here, and when it grows dark here, you have your dawn." And as night descended, Coyote heard whispers all around and saw that he was in a vast lodge, with many fires burning. He saw the door by which he had entered. Among the shadowy forms around him, he recognized many friends and his own dear wife.

All night long, Coyote greeted old companions. Toward dawn, the ghost warned Coyote that in daylight, the shadow world would fade away. "But stay here through your day, and in the evening you will see these people again." All day Coyote waited, hot and thirsty, on the prairie, until at sunset

he was again in the long lodge
and enjoyed himself all night.

Several days and nights went
by in this way, until the death
spirit told Coyote, "Tomor-
row you will start for home,
taking your wife with you. You
must be very careful. You will
travel for five days and cross
five mountains. You may talk
to your wife as you go, but
do not touch her until you have
crossed the last mountain."

Coyote left in the morning,
dimly sensing his wife's presence like a shadow behind
him. For four days they walked,
crossing one mountain each
day and camping at its base
in the evening, and each
day Coyote could see his wife
more clearly. On the fourth
night, with one more mountain
to cross, Coyote was suddenly overcome by the joy of seeing his beloved and stretched
out his arms to her. Mindful of
the ghost's warning, she cried,
"Do not embrace me!" But
Coyote rushed to her, and with
his touch, she vanished.

Immediately the death spirit
appeared, rebuking Coyote.
"You have spoiled everything,"
he said. "If you had carried out
this task, you would have fixed
the practice of returning from
death. Soon the human race is
coming and because you failed,
they will know death." And
though Coyote went back the
way he had gone with the
ghost, doing all they had done,
and found the spot in the prairie where the long house had
been, he never saw the lodge,
the ghost, his wife, or any
of the shadow people again.

Hare versus Trickster in a Deadly Game

Tricksters are clever, but they can be outwitted; they have special powers but are not all-powerful. As this Japanese story shows, although a trickster delights in fooling people and other animals, he may fall victim to another's prank—and even to his own foolishness.

An old country couple, so the story goes, had a pet white hare that they were very fond of. One day a tanuki—a small wild dog with eyepatches like a raccoon's—happened by and ate up the food that had been put out for the hare. Infuriated, the old man seized the tanuki, strung him up in a tree, and went off to cut wood, vowing to have roast tanuki for dinner. This tanuki, however, was a trickster and was not about to stay captured. Spying the old woman, the furry captive begged for his freedom, and the kind old soul released him. As soon as he was free, the tanuki ran away, screaming that he would get revenge.

This threat so alarmed the hare that he went in search of his master—a fruitless effort, as it happened. The tanuki, seeing his chance, crept back to the house and killed the woman, then took on her shape and made her corpse into a tasty meal. When the old man returned hungry from woodcutting, he gladly took a steaming bowl of stew from the figure he thought was his wife. But as he finished his lunch and expressed his enjoyment of it, the tanuki took back his own shape and taunted the man: 'You miserable wretch, you've

eaten your own wife—see, here are her old bones!" Laughing wickedly, the tanuki ran away.

Just then the hare arrived home and, learning the source of his master's grief, swore to avenge the murder of his mistress. He searched the woods until he found the tanuki laboring to carry a heavy load of firewood on his back. Quickly the hare set the wood afire; the tanuki, struggling under his burden, heard the crackling of the flames and asked the hare what the noise was. "These are the Crackling Mountains," replied the hare, "that sound is heard often hereabouts." By then flames were licking the tanuki's back, and he ran wailing to the river to douse them.

The hare followed, feigning sympathy and offering a plaster he said would soothe the tanuki's burns. But the plaster was made of hot red peppers, and as the tanuki howled in redoubled pain, the hare disappeared into the woods.

Once recovered, the tanuki set out to punish the hare and found him by the water, building a wooden boat. The hare said he was going to go in his boat to the moon and invited the tanuki along. The tanuki agreed to go but, mistrusting the hare, set about building his own boat—out of clay. They launched their boats, and of course the clay boat began to dissolve. As the water engulfed the frantic tanuki, the hare walloped him with an oar. The tanuki drowned, and the hare counted him paid in full for the murder of the old woman.

Children of the Wild

Close after the cubs came a hideous-looking creature—hand, foot and body like a human being. Close at its heels came another awful creature, exactly like the first, but smaller. Their eyes were bright and piercing, unlike human eyes. However, I at once came to the conclusion that they were human beings."

Thus did an Anglican priest in India describe his first glimpse, in 1920, of two girls he saw emerging with a family of wolves from their den. People have long been intrigued by such strange, often tragic, and frequently unconfirmed tales of feral—or wild—children, abandoned by humanity and reared by beasts. In 1758, Swedish botanist Carolus Linnaeus declared feral children a distinct species, *homo ferus*, distinguished by an inability to speak, an abundance of body hair, and the fact that they walked on all fours. Scientists have since dismissed this notion, attributing the children's unusual conduct to a severe emotional disorder. Amid all the lore of transformation between human and animal forms, feral children occupy a unique position: If the tales are true, they are humans who have experienced life as animals. No wonder their stories hold such a disturbing power.

Epitomizing the classic notion of feral children, mythical twins Romulus and Remus in this old bronze sculpture suckle at the dugs of the she-wolf who rescued and reared them.

The Wolf-Reared Founders of the Eternal City

Romulus and Remus, legendary sons of the war god Mars, were perhaps the world's foremost early examples of feral children. By order of the king of Alba Longa, who feared they would one day usurp his throne, the infant twins were cast adrift on the Tiber to die. The basket bearing the babies came to rest in reeds along the bank. There it was discovered by a she-wolf, an animal sacred to Mars, who suckled the children with her own milk. The boys grew up to found ancient Rome.

This myth set the pattern for tales of feral children. Wolves, for instance, have figured as the animal foster parents in the largest number of cases. One who followed in the Romulus-Remus tradition was the wolf-child of Hesse, Germany, allegedly discovered naked in the woods by hunters in 1344. The child's animal protectors, said the story, had raised him in a bed of earth lined with leaves. At night, the wolves warmed the boy with their bodies. Believed to be about four years of age when found by the men, he crawled about on all fours and favored raw meat. But unlike the legendary twins, the wolf-boy never became civilized. In hope of teaching him to walk upright, his keepers strapped boards to his legs, a painful, futile exercise. The boy eventually died, it was said, from eating rich and unfamiliar foods.

Many modern authorities reject all accounts of children reared by animals as unfounded in reality. Child psychologist Bruno Bettelheim sees them as examples of the "feral myth," reflecting a "desire to believe in a benign nature that in some fashion looks after all its children." This myth, he says, maintains that an animal and a human can be as close as a mother and her child.

It was that kind of cross-species bonding that was said to have

This eighteenth-century German etching was said to be a good likeness of Peter, Hamelin's wild boy.

A crudely drawn bear in Lithuania is seen nursing a human child among her own cubs in a seventeenth-century history book.

characterized a case that unfolded in Lithuania in 1661, when hunters found a forest-dwelling boy who showed every sign of having been raised by bears. The boy resisted capture with an animal's fury, using his sharp teeth and his clawlike nails. In captivity, he would not wear clothes or eat anything but meat and grass. He often slipped away from his caretakers to return to the woods, where he was once found embracing a savage bear. The boy was recaptured and, according to one account, was then confined in a convent.

Peter of Hamelin

One of the few feral children ever to enjoy even a modestly happy existence among his fellow humans was discovered running wild through a field near Hamelin, Germany, on July 27, 1724. Described as "naked, brownish, and black-haired," the creature was lured into town and captured by a man using apples as bait. Beneath the filth of the woods and a wild, matted mane of hair was a human boy about thirteen years old. It came to light that the child, called Peter, had been abandoned some time earlier by his father and stepmother, and although he did not appear to have had animal protectors, he had learned to survive in the wild.

Peter tolerated civilization only with great difficulty. He had little taste for cooked foods and tended to sniff with the air of a suspicious animal at anything offered to him. He preferred instead to strip the bark from green twigs and suck at the raw wood sap. Occasionally, he would trap and devour live birds.

In time, news of the wild boy circulated throughout Europe, and Peter subsequently served as the focus of several learned papers on the condition of the so-called natural man— that is, man with only "innate ideas," untouched by civilization. In 1726, the wild boy was presented before King George I of England. Peter adamantly refused the delicacies offered at the king's table, dining instead on raw, bloody meat.

Peter became more settled in old age; a small pension allowed him to live out his days on a peaceful farm in Hertfordshire. He even seemed to develop an appreciation for music, although he never advanced beyond the intelligence of a very backward child. In his almost six decades in human company, Peter never learned to speak more than a few words. In later life, his guardians rather cruelly hung a brass collar about his neck, bearing the inscription "Peter the Wild Boy," along with the address of the farm on which he lived. He died in 1785, at about age seventy-two.

Victor, the Wild Child of Aveyron

One of the strangest cases of a wild boy came to light in 1800, when a frightening creature was seen lurking near the farmhouses of Aveyron in southern France. Although the figure walked erect and wore the remains of a tattered shirt, his crouching movements and hairy appearance seemed more animal than human. Still, those who had seen him up close insisted he resembled a boy. The creature did not speak but sometimes uttered strange, inarticulate cries. He was captured twice but both times managed to escape.

After a third capture, the wild boy came to the attention of several scientists and physicians. Although he could hear, the wild boy seldom responded to humans. In time, he was sent to the Institute for Deaf-Mutes in Paris, where doctors declared him hopelessly retarded. Only one physician, Jean-Marc Gaspard Itard, offered any dissent. Itard believed that with intensive training the wild boy, whom he named Victor, might be tamed.

From the outset, it was obvious that conventional methods of teaching

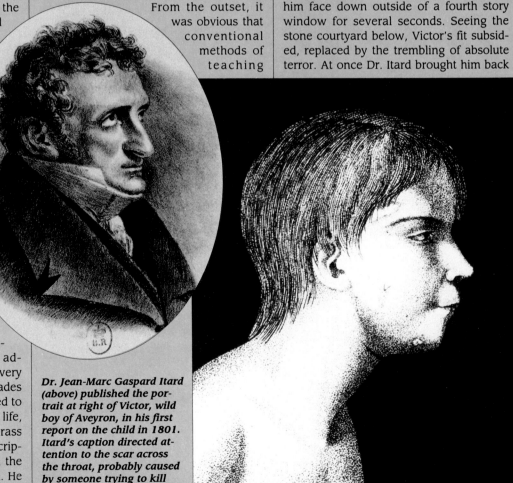

Dr. Jean-Marc Gaspard Itard (above) published the portrait at right of Victor, wild boy of Aveyron, in his first report on the child in 1801. Itard's caption directed attention to the scar across the throat, probably caused by someone trying to kill the boy in an act of cruelty.

would prove futile. The boy showed little interest in anything but food and sleep. Gradually, Itard learned to turn this to his advantage. He had played music for Victor with no response. He had tried to startle the boy with a gunshot, again drawing no reaction. But the sound of a walnut cracking—because it had to do with eating—evoked excited grunts.

Dr. Itard, therefore, tried to involve food in all his lessons. Hoping to improve the boy's concentration, Itard would hide a nut under one of three identical cups, then shuffle the cups in the manner of the shell-and-pea game. If Victor kept track of the proper cup, he would be given the nut. In time, the child came to enjoy the game and would play even without a reward. Over the course of a few days, the boy learned to use the word *lait,* for "milk," when milk was being poured. In time, he was even able to spell the word on wooden blocks.

During lessons the boy would sometimes fly into violent rages. In the midst of one of these outbursts, Dr. Itard took a radical step. Knowing that Victor had a fear of heights, he seized the boy and held him face down outside of a fourth story window for several seconds. Seeing the stone courtyard below, Victor's fit subsided, replaced by the trembling of absolute terror. At once Dr. Itard brought him back into the room, where, incredibly, the boy immediately resumed his lesson and completed the task at hand. Afterward, he threw himself on his bed and wept violently. So far as Dr. Itard knew, these were the first tears Victor had ever shed.

Still, efforts to tame the boy proved slow going. After five years, Victor's progress was sadly limited. Although he had grown less wild, his abilities remained slight. Dr. Itard reluctantly admitted that there were limits to man's ability to civilize a so-called wild child. He believed that a person's experiences and education formed that individual's very nature and personality and that a child such as Victor had never had the countless everyday experiences that contribute to humanity. Growing up in isolation, he concluded, rendered human beings inferior even to many animals, whose instincts left them better provided for life in the wild. "Without civilization," Itard wrote, "man would be one of the feeblest and least intelligent of animals."

For his own part, Victor offered no opinions on the matter. He lived out the remainder of his life in the care of a keeper, dying in 1828 near the age of forty.

Sanichar, the Wolf-Boy of India

Many reports of wolf-children have issued forth from India, where there are more wolves than in Europe and very few areas not occupied by humans. In early 1867, according to one account, a large band of hunters tracked a lone gray wolf to its lair in the jungles near Agra, in the north of India. There they came upon a wild crea-ture, human in shape but covered with filth, moving about on all fours with the motions of an animal. When the hunters attempted to capture the being, he fought back with a snarling fury, scratching and biting several men. Even when bound in chains, the ferocious creature continued to snap and lunge at the captors.

Realizing that they had bagged a human boy, the story continues, the hunters turned the child over to the Reverend C. S. Valentine, a missionary at Agra's Secundra Orphanage. Valentine found himself intrigued by the boy's plight. "Here," he wrote, "in an unfrequented jungle, running on all fours, covered with filth and vermin, his face partially hidden by long matted hair, and having no companion save the wolf, and no home save the wolf's den, was a boy, a boy who could not

After years in human company, India's wolf-boy Sanichar still reveals in this photograph the watchfulness of a wild animal. "His eyes," said his guardian, "glare, as if he expected an attack from some unseen enemy." At far left is a nineteenth-century artist's idealized notion of a wolf-child.

have been more than seven or eight years of age.'' Hoping to educate the child, Valentine named him Sanichar, Hindi for "Saturday," recalling the character of Friday, Robinson Crusoe's island companion.

The campaign to civilize Sanichar was not a great success. When the missionaries attempted to dress him, the boy would rip off the clothes and howl like a wild beast. He continued to prefer raw meat to cooked, tearing the food to shreds with teeth carefully sharpened on old bones. Gradually, however, Sanichar grew able to communicate with a limited form of sign language and learned to walk upright.

"In walking," Valentine observed, "he lifts his feet like one wading through wet

Soon after coming to their new orphanage home in India, wolf-girls Kamala and Amala "sleep like pigs when lying in a litter," said their guardian the Reverend J. A. L. Singh, "overlapping one another."

grass, and when he moves along the whole muscles of his body seem to be undergoing a series of jerks, while his arms are thrown about in such a manner as to convey the impression that they materially assist him in his progress. His head is also continually in motion, turning from side to side with great rapidity." Sanichar, it was said, lived out his life among the missionaries, dying in his mid-thirties in 1895.

The Man-Ghosts of Godamuri

Perhaps the most controversial feral-child case of the twentieth century is that of a pair of Indian wolf-girls called Amala and Kamala. The nine-year episode began in October 1920, in the jungles of Bengal. There, according to his own account, an Anglican missionary named J. A. L. Singh heard local villagers speaking fearfully of two horrifying *manush-baghas,* or "man-ghosts," having the form of human beings, but the heads of demons with bright, blazing eyes. The creatures had been sighted several times near a giant, abandoned ant heap seven miles from a village Singh identified as Godamuri.

When he took a hunting party out to investigate, Singh saw two ghostly figures, scurrying on all fours in the company of a wolf family. From his brief glimpse, the missionary believed that the strange figures must be human children. He concluded that the creatures lived within the anthill, coming and going through a hole in the side of the mound, and a few days afterward he organized a party of villagers to capture the mysterious beings.

While hunters stood by with bows and arrows, diggers and beaters surrounded the ant heap and began slapping at the walls with their shovels.

Immediately, Singh wrote later, two wolves sprang from the lair and broke through the cordon, fleeing into the surrounding woods. Then a third wolf, a female, jumped from the ant heap and raced at the men, gnashing her teeth and growling fiercely. It was obvious to the observers that she was protecting the creatures inside.

"I guessed from its whole bearing on the spot that it must have been the mother wolf, whose nature was so ferocious and affection so sublime," Singh recorded in his diary of the event. "I was simply amazed to think that an animal had such noble feeling surpassing even that of mankind. . . . Whoever these peculiar beings, and whatever they might be, certainly they were not [the wolf's] cubs, but had originally been brought as food for the cubs. To permit them to live, and to be nurtured by [the wolf] in this fashion, is divine." Unfortunately, Singh's revelation came too late to save the mother wolf. While making a second charge on the diggers, she was shot at close range by one of the archers. She died as soon as the arrow had pierced her side.

With the mother wolf killed, the tribesmen easily cut through the wall of the ant mound and found four creatures huddled within. Curled in a heap were two wolf cubs and the two man-ghost creatures Singh had sighted earlier. All four furiously resisted attempts to separate them, with the wolf-children struggling even more ferociously than the wolf cubs. Eventually, Singh ordered sheets thrown over them to help subdue them.

A brief examination revealed the creatures to be a pair of human girls, aged roughly two and eight years old. Singh decided to take them back to his orphanage in Midnapore and raise them as his own. He feared that if the story of this new discovery became widely known it would attract unwanted attention, endangering the girls' chances for a normal life. For a year, Singh and his wife kept the girls' origin a secret, preferring to try to raise them as they would any other orphans. The older

girl they named Kamala, and the younger one Amala.

After they were bathed and their tangled hair was cut, Amala and Kamala took on a more human appearance, but the task of domesticating them had only begun. In nearly all respects the children appeared to be totally wild. According to Singh, they crawled on their hands and knees, snarled viciously at human beings, and displayed a marked fear of daylight. And at night, he

A relatively docile-acting Kamala began to grow closer to her adopted parents, the Reverend and Mrs. J. A. L. Singh, following the death of her companion, Amala.

revealed, the girls would howl pitifully at the moon. They also sought raw meat, as had many others in the annals of feral children, sometimes using their keen sense of smell to scavenge chicken entrails from the garbage pail. But strangest of all, Singh went on, the girls' eyes gave off an eerie glow. "They had a peculiar blue glare," he noted, "like that of a cat or dog, in the dark. At night when you saw the glare, you could not see anything round about them but the two blue powerful lights . . . sending forth rays in the dark."

Within a year of their capture, both girls fell seriously ill, and despite the efforts of the local doctor, Amala, the younger child,

died of a kidney ailment. Although neither girl had ever shown the slightest trace of human emotion, Kamala wept at her companion's passing. But even as her tears flowed, her face remained strangely impassive. Still, the girl's death brought about a major change in Kamala. Slowly, she assumed a few human characteristics, dressing herself in clothes and even learning to speak a few words. In time, she began to walk upright for short distances.

These few human traits seemed to signal a transformation of Kamala's very character. The child who had once had an aversion to daylight now became afraid of the dark. And the Singhs' dog, whom Kamala had befriended and whose food she had sometimes shared, took to barking at her, as it would at any unfamiliar person.

In 1929, Kamala died at about age seventeen, of the same type of kidney ailment that had killed Amala. By then, Kamala's story had become public, and her death did little to quiet the interest and controversy that Singh had sought to avoid. Twenty-two years later, in 1951, an American sociologist named William F. Ogburn traveled to India to study the case. Even with the aid of a detective agency, he could not verify Singh's account of the capture of the girls. In fact, he could not even locate the village of Godamuri, where the episode was supposed to have taken place. Singh himself had died in the interim and could not defend himself against charges that he had fabricated the entire tale.

But in 1975 another researcher, Charles Maclean, tracked down a man claiming to be a member of Singh's original hunting party, who supported the missionary's account. Maclean concluded that although Singh may have exaggerated some details, he had basically reported the truth.

Even so, the story of Kamala and Amala soon became a battleground among psychologists. Dr. Arnold Gesell, of Yale University's Clinic of Child Development, found ample evidence to support Singh's record of Kamala's behavior. "Kamala was subjected in turn to three great crises," he wrote. "She was bereft of human care when she was carried to a den of wolves; she was bereft of the hard-won securities

of her wolf life when she was 'rescued' by
hunters who shot her foster mother. . . .
Finally she was pitifully bereft of the secu-
rity of reminiscent kinship and compan-
ionship when her younger wolf-child sister
Amala died so early.'' Dr. Gesell found it
remarkable that under these hardships Kamala showed any human development
at all, pointing out that the emotional
obstacles in the girl's path were all but in-
surmountable.

Child psychologist Dr. Bruno Bettelheim,
in his subsequent study of the case, came
to an entirely different conclusion. Bettelheim noted a similarity between the recorded symptoms of a number of so-called
feral children and the actions of young-
sters in his care who suffered from autism,
a mental disturbance characterized by
wild behavior and withdrawal from contact with the world. In his laboratory, Bettelheim had watched as clean and properly
clothed autistic children had become
snarling, violent savages, sometimes in a
matter of minutes. In some cases, autistic
children evinced a peculiar craving for raw
meat. The psychologist believed that many
alleged feral children were actually autistic. Perhaps, he speculated, these apparently wild creatures had become so
unmanageable that their parents had
abandoned them or allowed them to wander off. The very notion of children being
raised by wild animals, he concluded,
might well prove a myth created by adults
to account for this animalistic behavior.

Cavorting with Gazelles

Certainly some modern reports of feral
children lack credible provenances, while
others have the earmarks of outright fabri-
cation. Among the former was the story of
a gazelle-boy allegedly discovered in Syria
in the mid-1940s. Without making any
claims for the tale's authenticity but pre-
senting it as hearsay, a French author
named André Demaison related it in 1953
in a volume titled *Le Livre des Enfants Sauvages* ("The Book of Wild Children"). According to accounts Demaison had heard,
the boy, about ten years old, had developed powerful muscles that enabled him
to run and jump almost as swiftly as the
gazelles among which he was found. The
story said pursuers were able to capture

the boy only after they chased him across the desert with an army jeep.

Entrusted to the care of public assistance authorities in Damascus, the gazelle-boy allegedly resisted all attempts to civilize him and tried several times to escape. According to another source, in one dramatic break for freedom, the child leaped from a window and created a panic as he lunged wildly through the crowded streets. By this account, his overseers recaptured him and then surgically mutilated his Achilles tendons to prevent his running away again. Researchers who have looked into the story have found no clues to what supposedly happened to the boy nor any documentary evidence to substantiate the account.

A French poet and artist named Jean-Claude Armen discovered a gazelle-boy of his own in 1960—or so he claimed in a book published in 1971. Armen said he was traveling through Western Sahara when he spotted a herd of gazelles run-ning swiftly across the horizon. For an in-stant before the animals disappeared from view, he thought he caught a glimpse of a human child among them. Later, he said, he came upon a cluster of hoofprints in the sand and found among them the clear imprints of little human feet.

Armen followed the tracks, he said, to a small oasis in the side of a mountain. Here, as the animals took food and water, he got his first clear look at the gazelle-boy, tearing at a plant root with his teeth. "The child, now clearly visible, shows his lively, dark, almond-shaped eyes and a pleasant, open expression," Armen wrote in his journal. "He appears to be about ten years old, his ankles are disproportionately thick and obviously powerful, his muscles firm and shivering." Fascinated, Armen resolved to win the herd's trust and study the boy's life among the animals. For days at a time, Armen sat quietly at a distance, allowing the herd to grow accustomed to his scent. Gradually, the younger gazelles began sniffing and licking his feet and hands. In time, the rest of the herd followed.

At last, the gazelle-boy himself approached. As the child drew near, Armen noted that he wrinkled up his nose and face in the manner of a gazelle catching a scent. Eventually the boy grew at ease with the visitor, even licking Armen's hands as the gazelles had done.

Armen stayed to observe the herd for several weeks. The boy, Armen saw, followed the same strict code of conduct that applied to all members of the herd and fed on the same diet of plant roots. On occasion, when food became exceptionally scarce, the boy would capture and devour a desert lizard.

After a few weeks, Armen's supplies ran out, and he left to return to France. But he remained intrigued by the gazelle-boy, and two years later he returned to Western Sahara, accompanied by two French army officers—neither of whom ever came forward to confirm his story. Nearing the oasis where he had first approached the gazelle-boy, Armen caught sight of the herd. The boy, taller

A sketch from the journal of Jean-Claude Armen conveys the French artist's idealized view of the boy he claimed to have found frolicking with gazelles in Western Sahara.

and stronger looking, was among them.

As Armen renewed his efforts to win the youngster's trust, the army officers grew restless. While driving near the oasis late one afternoon, one of the officers decided to test the boy's speed with his jeep. Over Armen's objections, he gunned his engine and flushed the herd, with the boy among them, out onto the desert. With Armen clinging to the windshield, the jeep jolted along the hard sand and rock while the gazelles zigzagged wildly, trying to escape. The gazelle-boy, his eyes wide with fear, bounded ahead with giant leaps as the jeep gained on him. Then, said Armen, at a speed of thirty-three miles per hour one of the jeep's tires blew out, throwing the occupants on the ground as the boy vanished from sight. Armen never saw him again.

Armen's early reports possessed a certain plausibility and created much interest in the academic world. He induced a distinguished French zoologist, Professor Théodore Monod, to write a foreword for his book about the gazelle-boy, giving the work a kind of scientific stamp of approval. But when Monod later pressed for proof of the discovery, Armen was elusive. "Every time I tried to obtain a precise piece of evidence," said Monod, "I never got anywhere with him." When, after many requests, Armen sent Monod a photograph of the alleged gazelle-boy, "it was nothing more than a retouched version of the famous picture of the gazelle-boy found in Syria." Acknowledging he had no photo of the boy, Armen then sent what he said were pictures of the gazelles—but Monod knew instantly they were of a gazelle species not found in Western Sahara. Monod

finally concluded that Armen was "a man of great imagination."

Life among the Apes

Skepticism of scientific authorities notwithstanding, there has been no shortage of feral-child reports this century. In 1903, a boy who appeared to be about twelve years old was supposedly captured among a tribe of baboons in the Koonap District of South Africa. The child reportedly displayed many baboon characteristics: He made incessant chattering noises, jerked his head and scratched like the animal, and moved with a four-legged, loping gait. When a stay in a mental hospital showed that he possessed normal intelligence, he

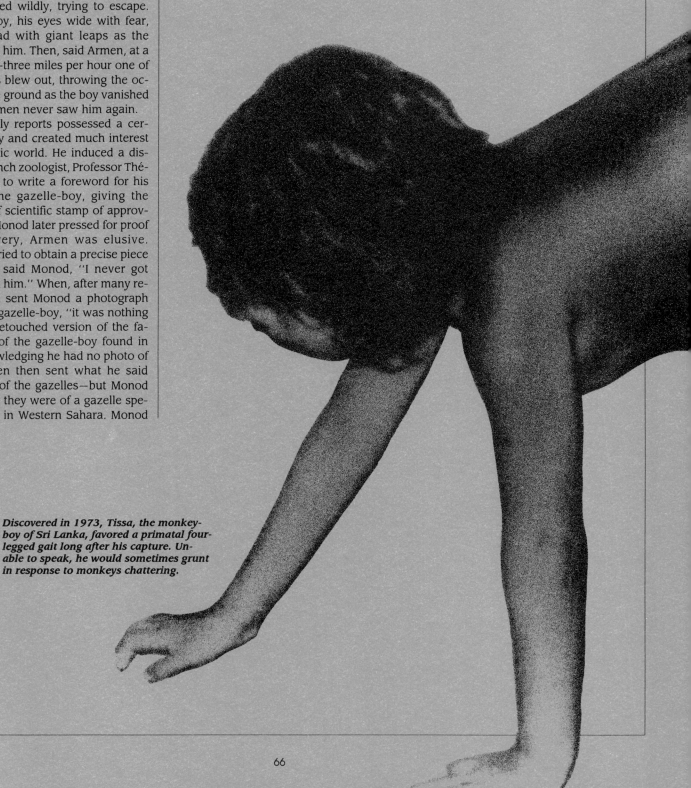

Discovered in 1973, Tissa, the monkey-boy of Sri Lanka, favored a primatal four-legged gait long after his capture. Unable to speak, he would sometimes grunt in response to monkeys chattering.

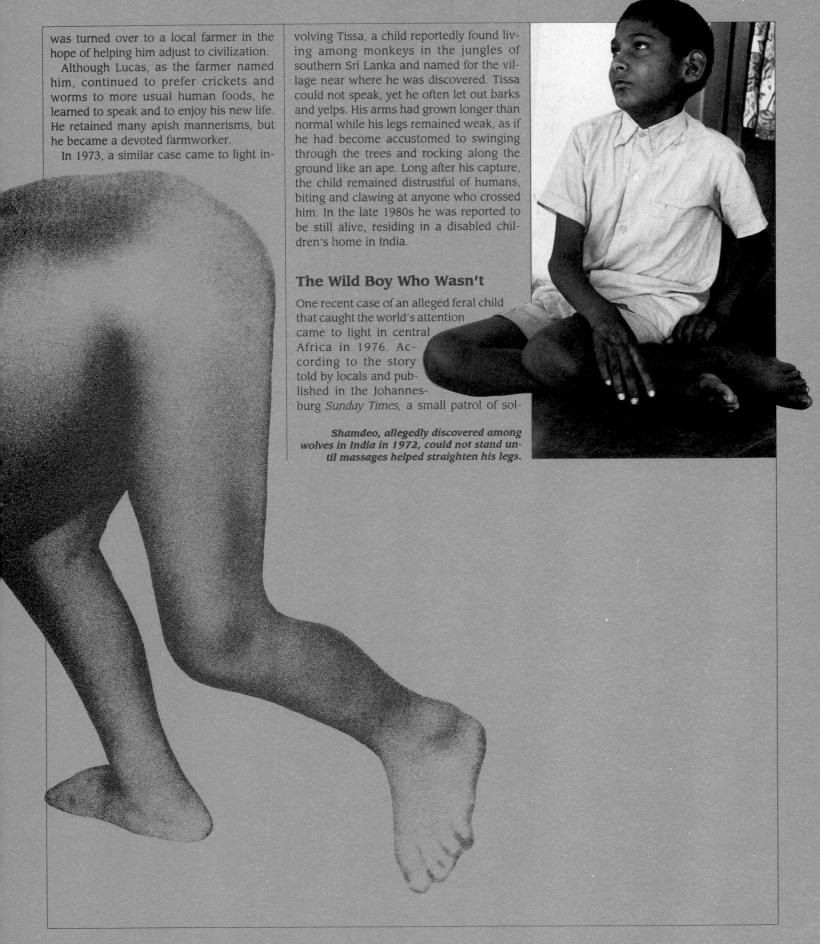

was turned over to a local farmer in the hope of helping him adjust to civilization.

Although Lucas, as the farmer named him, continued to prefer crickets and worms to more usual human foods, he learned to speak and to enjoy his new life. He retained many apish mannerisms, but he became a devoted farmworker.

In 1973, a similar case came to light involving Tissa, a child reportedly found living among monkeys in the jungles of southern Sri Lanka and named for the village near where he was discovered. Tissa could not speak, yet he often let out barks and yelps. His arms had grown longer than normal while his legs remained weak, as if he had become accustomed to swinging through the trees and rocking along the ground like an ape. Long after his capture, the child remained distrustful of humans, biting and clawing at anyone who crossed him. In the late 1980s he was reported to be still alive, residing in a disabled children's home in India.

The Wild Boy Who Wasn't

One recent case of an alleged feral child that caught the world's attention came to light in central Africa in 1976. According to the story told by locals and published in the Johannesburg *Sunday Times*, a small patrol of sol-

Shamdeo, allegedly discovered among wolves in India in 1972, could not stand until massages helped straighten his legs.

diers was forging its way through a tropical forest in Burundi in 1974 when it came upon a group of gray enkende monkeys. As the creatures scattered into the surrounding trees, one of the soldiers noticed a particular monkey that displayed far less agility than its companions. It clung desperately to the trunk of a tree, chattering angrily and making little progress in its climb. As the soldier drew nearer, he realized that the creature was a small human boy.

The soldiers captured the child, according to the account, and in time the boy was brought to a nearby missionary. There it was decided that he should be named John, after John the Baptist, who had also wandered for a time in the wilderness. Poor nutrition had stunted the child's growth, and although his stature made him appear about four years old, his large head led doctors to conclude that he was actually several years older. John seemed to be a textbook case of a human raised in the wild. He walked on all fours, made no sounds except for his monkeylike chattering, and had a coating of fine, dark hair covering his body. Doctors held out little hope of educating the boy. Although he learned to walk upright, he showed almost no other human traits and very limited intelligence.

Publicity about the case soon attracted the attention of a pair of American college professors, psychologist Harlan Lane and psychiatrist Richard Pillard. Lane, who had earlier written a book about Victor, the wild boy of Aveyron, could not resist the chance to study a modern-day feral child.

In May 1976, Lane and Pillard flew to Africa in order to meet the monkey-boy face to face. Lane's journal of their first encounter with John shows that the boy appeared, to the psychologist, to be the very picture of a wild child. "He is sitting cross-legged on the floor," Lane wrote, "eating with his fingers from a plate of food in front of him. Certainly he is a strange-looking child. From where I stand, nearly in front of him, I cannot see his pupils, only the whites of his eyes; his gaze is fixed rigidly off to the extreme right. His lips are pulled back over his teeth in an expression of pain or fear. His right hand flaps relentlessly up and down in front of his face, fingers splayed. He chatters con-

stantly, his lips and cheeks vibrating to make bizarre—yes, monkey-like—sounds; he occasionally breaks into a screech while his body rocks back and forth."

Both professors hoped that they had at last come across an authentic, definitive case of a human reared in the wild. From this promising first impression, however, their investigation quickly ran aground. As part of their probe, the men showed a photograph of John to the staff of various local orphanages, including one in Bujumbura. It was here that a supervisor

recognized John as a mentally retarded patient named Balthazar, whose parents had died by the time he was about a year old. Lane and Pillard soon deduced that John was actually an autistic child shifted from one orphanage to another in infancy until his records and true identity became lost. In short time, this theory proved correct. The entire tale of the wild boy of Burundi, it appeared, was little more than an elaborate concoction spread by local folk for the pleasure of the telling.

Although they had come a long way only to meet disappointment, Lane and Pillard clung to the hope that a genuine feral-child case one day would surface. Feral children, they believed, might well hold clues to the evolution of human intelligence. And in any case, simply to communicate with one who had developed in a natural state, unshaped by civilization, held promise of fascination in and of itself. Nearly two centuries earlier, a French philosopher had voiced a similar feeling about the wild child called Victor of Aveyron. ''I would rather spend one hour with this boy,'' he had written, ''than one week with the finest minds in Europe.''

It was later discovered that ''John, the jungle boy of Burundi,'' had lived in orphanages, not with apes, but sensationalized press accounts at first labeled him a ''real-life Tarzan.''

CHAPTER 2

Werewolves

hrough much of the last quarter of the sixteenth century, a large wolf rampaged the countryside around the German towns of Cologne and Bedburg. Its attacks on townsfolk and their animals were so frequent and its victims so numerous that people feared to travel from one place to another alone. "Oftentimes," recounted a lurid 1591 pamphlet, "the Inhabitants found the Armes & legges of dead Men, Women, and Children scattered up and down the feelds to their great greefe and vexation of hart." But try as they might, they could not catch and kill "this greedy and cruell Woolfe."

Then, as chance would have it, a group of men spotted the wolf, surrounded him, "and most circumspectlye set their Dogges upon him, in such sort that there was no means to escape." To their astonishment the wolf turned out not to be an animal at all, but a man, one Peter Stubbe, well known to the very people whose friends and children he had murdered. Stubbe, according to the pamphlet, was that most feared of creatures, a werewolf, changed by magic from man to beast and driven to wantonly kill and feast on his human victims.

Stubbe's case contains so many classic elements of the werewolf phenomenon that it is worth examining in some detail. Tied by his captors to the torture device known as the wheel and fearing the punishment they would use to force his story out of him, he confessed to a series of villainies. He revealed how he achieved his transformation into ravener by strapping around his waist a magic girdle or belt, "procured of the Devill." Thus equipped, he became, as the pamphlet delighted in telling, "strong and mighty, with eyes great and large, which in the night sparkeled like unto brandes of fire, a mouth great and wide, with most sharpe and cruell teeth, a huge body, and mightye pawes." Unable to find the girdle, the magistrates assumed that the devil had reclaimed it after abandoning Stubbe "to the torments which his deedes deserved."

And heinous deeds they were. Among his reported victims were thirteen children and two pregnant women, from whose wombs he tore their babies and eaten the "harts panting hot and rawe, which he accounted dainty morsells & best agreeing to his Appetite."

Such crimes were so outside ordinary human experience that they gripped the imagination of the public and served to stoke the fears of those nervous souls who believed that werewolves existed everywhere and must be eradicated at all costs. That Stubbe was villain through and through there was no doubt, according to the pamphlet. "Greatly inclined to evill" from his earliest youth, he had begun practicing the black arts when he was only twelve years old, and sorcery soon became such an obsession with him that, it was said, he was willing to make a pact with the devil for power. In return Stubbe received the instrument of his downfall, the magic girdle, which he wore at first to take revenge on his enemies, real or imagined. Attacking them wherever he found them, in the country or the city, he pounced on them in the form of a wolf and would "never rest till he had pluckt out their throates" and had torn their joints asunder.

Once, for instance, Stubbe spotted two men and a woman walking along the road that ran through the forest where he hid. He called out to one of the men, whom he knew, and the man went into the woods. When he did not return, his companion followed, and this man, too, disappeared. The woman fled, but not quickly enough. The alleged werewolf raped and murdered her. The men's mangled bodies were later found in the forest. The woman's body, however, never reappeared. It is believed that Stubbe had devoured it.

As his bloodthirstiness grew, it is said, Stubbe took to walking the fields night and day in search of victims. If he spotted some young girls playing together or milking their cows, for instance, he would run among them, swifter than any greyhound, and seize one to rape and murder while the others fled.

It remains unclear whether Stubbe ever married, but he did have a mistress, a woman "of tall and comely stature, of exceeding good favour and one that was well esteemed among her neighbors." He also consorted with a variety of other women. Somewhere along the line he fathered two children, a boy and a girl. As his daughter grew older, she became increasingly beautiful, and Stubbe took a fancy to her. "And such was his filthye desire toward her," breathlessly states the pamphlet describing his life, "that he begat a Childe by her, dayly using her as his Concubine." Nor was his incest limited to his daughter: He bedded his sister as well.

If there was one person Stubbe loved, it was his son, whom he affectionately called his heart's ease. But even here his pleasure in brutality and gore so exceeded the joy he derived from the child that he "inticed him into the feeldes, and from thence into a Forrest hard by, and there most cruelly slewe him, which doon, he presently eat the brains out of his head." At this, the pamphlet explodes in outrage, condemning the murder as "the most monstrous act that ever man heard off, for never was knowen a wretch from nature so far degenerate."

No punishment, however monstrous it might be in its own right, could fit the magnitude of Stubbe's crimes. His body was laid on the wheel and his flesh pulled off the bones in several places with "red hotte burning pincers." Then his arms and legs were broken. Finally his head was "strook from his body," reserved, and his carcass burned to ashes. As accessories to the murders, his daughter and mistress were incinerated alive.

After the executions, the magistrates had a grim monument reared in the town of Bedburg. Workmen set the wheel on which Stubbe had been broken atop a tall pole and affixed his head to it. To serve as a reminder of the animal guise he had supposedly assumed on his murderous forays, they included the carved likeness of a wolf, and to commemorate his victims, they suspended from the rim of the wheel pieces of yard-long wood in a number equal to the sixteen poor souls he had admitted to murdering. Word of Stubbe's lycanthropy spread far and wide, and his sensational story was told and retold so many times, by so many different people, that his name eventually became distorted in the telling, appearing in the various surviving sources as Stumpf, Stube, and Stub.

Dusty archives the world over contain records telling of pathetic werewolves such as Stubbe, compelled to abandon their humanity for the bestial appearance and behavior of the wolf. This animal—a creature of cunning, stealth, swiftness, and rapacity—was the one most often described in stories of lycanthropy. Perhaps it caught the imagination because throughout much of human history, wolf packs were a real menace to men and women: Their depradations were a cause for serious alarm among people who lived in villages and on farms. Even to this day, stories occasionally crop up in the press about wolves that, driven by hunger, attack people in Europe and the Middle East.

Faced with these powerful predators, people made them part of their lore; dangerous, powerful humans were thought to assume the characters of the animals. Sometimes it was only behavior that was wolflike. Romulus and Remus, the legendary twins who founded Rome, for instance, were said to have been suckled by a she-wolf—and to have acquired her ferocity as a result. The tradition was echoed in the customs of the Roman infantry, organized and disciplined in the manner of a wolf pack and all but unstoppable. According to the historian Polybius, those Roman soldiers who displayed conspicuous bravery in battle were allowed to wear wolf skins. Cowards were torn to pieces by their peers.

Sometimes, however, wolfish behavior was seen not as mere imitation but as actual transformation of human into beast. Centuries ago, this was said to occur through the will of the gods, through sorcery, or through the use of magical drugs. Later writers attributed lycanthropy to various paranormal causes or considered it hallucination induced by mania or by physical disease.

The intensity of the attention directed at this kind of shapeshifting indicated the enormous attraction the belief aroused—and still arouses. Werewolf legends are profitably exploited by Hollywood. And, obviously, some people believe them: In 1988, the Fox Broadcasting Company instituted a six-week-long Werewolf Hotline. It received more than 340,000 telephone calls from viewers reporting sightings of werewolves and blaming the creatures for various unsolved murders lingering on police blotters.

From centuries of stories, a composite portrait can be assembled of the werewolf. In human form, it tended to

A quarter century of rape, murder, and incest near Cologne, Germany, came to a halt with the capture and the trial (right) of alleged werewolf Peter Stubbe, depicted in the sixteenth-century woodcuts here and the ones showing his punishment on the following pages. Stubbe attributed his ghostly transformation to a pact with the devil.

have bushy eyebrows that met over the bridge of the nose; red teeth; a long third finger; long, almond-shaped fingernails, with a blood-red tinge to them; and ears that tended to be far back and low down on the head. The person's mouth and eyes were dry, and he was often thirsty. (According to one French judge who regularly attended torture sessions, werewolves, like witches, were unable to weep.) The skin was scabrous, much scratched and cut because of the brush through which the werewolf ran in animal form, and often of a yellowish, pinkish, or greenish cast, with a tendency to hairiness. One man, who apparently did not have a hairy body but considered himself a werewolf nonetheless, insisted that his hair grew inward, beneath the skin; to test this, his interrogators flayed him here and there and, finding nothing, turned him over to a surgeon for treatment. Not surprisingly, he soon died.

In addition to such physical features, the werewolf displayed certain pronounced psychological traits. Among these was a preference for night over day and solitude to company. Beset by deep melancholy ("very black and vehement," as the late-seventeenth-century French historian Simon Goulert describes it), the person was a habitué of graveyards and was known, on occasion, to dig up a corpse

and feast on it. February was apparently the cruelest month for a lycanthrope, or at least so suggests Tommaso Garzoni in his *Hospitall of Incurable Fooles,* published in 1600. There, Garzoni tells how in the months of February the lycanthrope "will goe out of the house in the night like a wolfe, hunting about the graves of the dead with great howling, and plucke the dead mens bones out of the sepulchers, carrying them about the streets, to the great fears and astonishment of all them that meet him." Goulert describes running into one of his friends, a lycanthrope, who deep in a melancholy fit carried "upon his shoulders the whole thigh and the legge of a dead man."

The transformation of the afflicted human into a beast was supposedly achieved in a number of ways. It was said that, like witches, werewolves rubbed their bodies with magic ointments and salves of various kinds. The composition of these differed, but many contained psychoactive alkaloids that had potent hallucinatory effects, which could lead to a belief that the body had changed. Indeed, two of the most commonly employed plant ingredients in lycanthropy's pharmacopoeia—nightshade and henbane—could produce in the person who had absorbed them through the skin or taken them by mouth the delusion that he or she

had become a wolf. Pig fat, turpentine, and olive oil were among the substances used as a base for such a salve. Later, when the distillation of spirits was perfected, alcohol was used as a solvent for the herbs. Extracted into a potion, they became even more active.

Helping the delusion along was the wolf hide or the girdle or belt made from the animal's skin that the aspiring werewolf often wore. To further increase the efficacy of the ointments and potions, magical incantations were also frequently used. Chanted in the manner of prayer, from within the confines of a magic circle traced in soil, these required a practiced and reverent delivery in order to be effective *(pages 95-103).*

These medieval rituals, however, came late in werewolf lore. They were said to have been used by those who wished to become werewolves. In the earliest of stories, lycanthropy was the result not of a wish but of a curse. Such a tale is the Greek myth of Lycaon. In one version of this legend, the great shapeshifter Zeus, disguised this time as a wayfarer, sought hospitality at the court of a vicious Arcadian king named Lycaon. Lycaon, recognizing the god and attempting to kill him, served a dish containing human

flesh. But omnipotent Zeus recognized the terrible trick and did not eat. Outraged, he drove Lycaon from his palace, destroyed it, and as a final punishment, exiled the king to the countryside, damning him to live out the rest of his life as a wolf, the animal he most resembled.

A vivid description of his metamorphosis was given in later centuries by Ovid, the Roman poet. Lycaon's "clothes changed into bristling hairs, his arms to legs. His own savage nature showed in his rabid jaws, and he now directed against the flocks his innate lust for killing. He had a mania, even yet, for shedding blood. But though he was a wolf, he retained some traces of his original shape. The grayness of his hair was the same, his face showed the same violence, his eyes gleamed as before, and he presented the same picture of ferocity."

The tale was only one expression of a violent Arcadian tradition. According to ancient historians, transformations involving human sacrifices were carried out in the Arcadian temple on Mount Lycaeus, in whose holy precincts neither man nor woman was supposed ever to cast a shadow or to remain alive for more than a year. The sacrifices were the means by which cultists were transformed into

wolves. It was said that such transformations lasted nine years only—unless the animals ate human flesh. Then they were doomed to remain beasts forever.

With Ovid's tale the werewolf tradition entered popular literature, which provided plenty of eerie accounts. The Roman Petronius, for instance, regaled his readers with the story of a former slave named Niceros. One night, this young man left Rome to visit his mistress, who lived on a farm some miles from the city. He persuaded a soldier—"as lusty a lad as the very devil"—to keep him company on the road. "Off we set about cockcrow," related Niceros, "and the moon was shining as bright as midday." When they passed a cemetery, the soldier turned off the road and walked among the monuments, apparently to relieve himself. But to Niceros's surprise, his companion took off all his clothes and left them in a pile by the roadside. Stranger still, he urinated in a circle, which held some magic import, for within minutes he turned into a wolf. Howling, the moon-struck soldier ran off into the woods. The startled Niceros tried to pick up the man's clothes but found that they had turned to stone.

"Half dead with fear," Niceros made his way in the darkness to the house of his mistress, whom he found in an agitated state of mind. If only he had come a little earlier, she said, he could have helped. A wolf had broken into the barnyard and wreaked havoc among the cows and sheep. But the marauder had not escaped unwounded, she was happy to say; one of the farmhands had managed to jab it in the neck with a pike.

After staying the night, Niceros started back to his master's. When he came to the spot where the rigidified clothes had lain, he found a pool of blood. And when he got home, he discovered the soldier lying in bed, attended by a doctor who was busy dressing a wound in his neck. Niceros needed no more confirmation than this of his friend's supernatural power, "and after that I could neither bite nor sup with him; no, not if you had killed me for it." Wound doubling—a phenomenon in which a wound appeared on a lycanthrope in both its animal and human form—was believed, then and later, to be a sure sign of a werewolf.

The folk tradition of werewolf tales was as widespread in medieval Europe as it was in the classical world. Certain peoples of Poland and Lithuania, for instance, were widely regarded as sorcerers who, it was said, turned themselves temporarily into wolves once a year. The stories clung to the region for centuries, as is suggested by a Latvian court record dating from 1555 in which a man "who was never known to lack common sense," confessed how he and other peasants had gone into the bush, taken off their clothes together, and instantly become wolves. "In that shape," notes the document, "they tore apart whatever animals they could encounter," including horses and cattle.

Such ritualistic transformation seems to be echoed in the tales of Livonia (now part of the Soviet Union's Estonian and Latvian republics) describing ceremonies occurring during the Christmas season; Christmas, because of its association with the winter solstice, was traditionally a period of magical activity of all kinds. According to one such legend—recorded in the sixteenth century—thousands of villagers from the region were forced on December 26 to fol-

In the grisly custom of the day, Peter Stubbe's punishment truly fit his confessed crimes. He was strapped to a wheel, torn apart with hot pincers, and finally decapitated. Stubbe's headless body was joined at the stake by his mistress and daughter, who were judged both victims of and accomplices to his crimes.

The Noble Life of the Real Wolf

The term *werewolf* reflects humankind's traditional attitude toward the wolf itself, long feared as a killer of men, women, and children. The real wolf, however, turns out to be a more benign creature than most people imagine. Although studies in the wild have shown it to be a fierce hunter, the wolf also has a social organization and family life to touch the heart.

Wolves are organized by packs that usually have no more than twenty members. Each animal occupies his or her own place in a strict hierarchy, with a strong, aggressive male serving as leader, or alpha male; an alpha female dominates the females. Since each pack must operate as a unit, especially on the hunt, discipline works to the good of all. Each wolf knows its position and role. Rank is indicated by how high a wolf carries its tail; the alpha male carries his tail higher than any of the others.

Protective of its territory, the pack marks key points along the boundaries with urine to discourage the intrusion of other packs and uses the famous wolf call to further warn interlopers away. Since a territory may cover as much as 4,000 square miles, the call also lets scattered members stay in touch with one another over long distances, as the lone Canadian wolf here is doing.

On the hunt, a pack can cover up to forty-five miles a day and can go without food for as long as two weeks. When prey is sighted *(opposite, top),* the members cooperate until the animal is brought down. The leading male and female then feed first while the

other members patiently wait their turn according to their rank; the lowest ranking wolf often gets only scraps.

The lowest ranking wolf is the scapegoat of the pack, forced to endure unprovoked attacks from other members and frequently relegated to the fringe of the pack's territory. These so-called omega animals may be ostracized because they are victims of diseases that threaten the health of the pack or because they are deposed alpha wolves, past their prime. If driven from the territory of the pack entirely, this animal becomes the lone wolf humans have come to fear—albeit needlessly, since single animals are very ineffective hunters against large prey such as livestock. In time the lone wolf may meet up with an outcast of the opposite sex and begin to establish a new pack in unoccupied territory.

Wolves generally mate for life and are solicitous of their offspring, the whole pack helping in the pups' care and raising. After feeding on prey, the hunters return to the denning area and there disgorge meat for the young to eat, whether they are the parents or not. This is an efficient delivery system: Wolves can carry as much as ten pounds of meat in their stomachs. Each may bury for its own later use some of the food that it brings back.

Much of what has been learned about wolves in North America runs directly counter to the animal's traditional bad reputation in the Old World *(pages 80-81).* The difference may be attributed to a number of factors. For centuries, wolves in Europe lived in closer proximity to human populations than wolves in the more spacious wilds of America. Thus the European wolf seeking food and territory was more likely to collide with humans with similar aims. Also, some European wolves may have been driven by rabies to bite human victims. Others may have mated with dogs and produced powerful hybrid offspring with more vicious characteristics, such as the fearsome animals that attacked more than 100 peasants in late-eighteenth-century France. But in North America, no healthy wolf has ever been known to attack a human.

Out hunting, a pack goes for the kill (upper right). The lead male can be seen in the foreground with his tail upright. When it comes time to consume the prey (lower right), a musk oxen calf that became separated from its mother, the lead male feeds first, in the company of the alpha female. Days may pass before the blood will disappear from his muzzle.

low a mysterious crippled boy into the countryside. These slaves of Satan, as they were called, were transformed into ravening wolves that fell upon grazing cattle and other livestock in an orgy of rioting that continued for twelve days. After that, the victims regained their human forms, falling on the ground as though taken with a sudden illness, and they remained "motionless and extended like corpses, deprived of all feeling." Unfortunately, what happened next was never recorded.

Ireland was a similar repository of werewolf lore, perhaps because wolves thrived there long after they were hunted to extinction in England. At one time the Emerald Isle was even known as wolf-land, and the formidable Irish wolfhound—"bigger of bone and limme than a colt," as one sixteenth-century writer expressed it—was bred into existence to combat its namesake. Saint Patrick himself was believed to have transformed Vereticus, the king of Wales, into a wolf.

Where the truth ends and fantasy begins in such accounts is impossible to say. But romanticized stories involving werewolves would persist for years in Europe, suggesting a large audience more than willing to believe in shapeshifting. England's Gervase of Tilbury, a scholastic writing between 1210 and 1214, noted that "in England we often see men changed into wolves at the changes of the moon." Gervase's *Otia Imperialia,* a collection of medieval legends and superstitions, includes the tale of Raimbaud of Auvergne, a former soldier turned outlaw. Exiled to the forests, Raimbaud turned into a werewolf and began a series of attacks on children and adults alike. His predations continued until he assaulted a carpenter, who chopped off one of his hind paws, whereupon he suddenly reverted to human shape. According to the story, Raimbaud thanked his intended victim for ridding him "for ever of the accursed and damned form." This led Gervase to add a bit of werewolf lore: "It is commonly reported and held by grave and worthy doctors that if a werewolf be shorn of one of his members, he shall surely recover his original body."

Out of Ireland comes a similarly curious twelfth-century werewolf tale. In his *Topographia Hiberniae* (Irish Topography), the ecclesiastic Gerald of Wales related the tale of a priest and a boy traveling from Ulster toward Meath. They stopped one night in an unfamiliar forest and kindled a fire beneath a large tree, and presently a wolf approached, speaking in a human voice. "Do not alarm yourselves, do not in any way be afraid." The well-spoken wolf then unfolded his sad story.

He was a man, he said, who with his wife had lived in the ancient kingdom of Ossory in southwest Leinster. The kingdom, for reasons not specified, lay under a curse: Every seven years, a pair of villagers were doomed to throw off human form and live as wolves. If they survived the ordeal, they could resume their natural shapes after the seventh year and return to their homes, and another couple had to take their place. He and his wife had served part of the sentence, said the wolf, but now she lay ill, possibly dying. His story told, he turned to the priest and added, "I beseech you of your good charity to comfort her with the aid of your priestly office"—that is, to give her the last rites, that she might die as a Christian.

The priest agreed to do this and with the boy followed the wolf deep into the woods, where they found the she-wolf hidden in the hollow of a tree, groaning with "sad human sighs." Though willing to administer the last rites, the priest was reluctant to offer an animal the consecrated Host—until the wolf, with his claws, drew the pelt back from his wife's head, folding it down to reveal the body of an old woman. When the priest's prayers were finished, the wolf led him and the boy back to their camp and in the morning escorted them safely from the forest. What became of the animals the story did not go on to relate. As if to vouch for the truth of the matter, however, Gerald claimed that accounts of the incident were taken to Rome to be examined by the pope himself.

From such gossipy accounts as Gerald's and Gervase's, as well as from folk tales, medieval writers of romance constructed airy fictions. Werewolves figured in wicked-stepmother and lost-heir stories and, in one case, in a tale of cruel infidelity.

This was the *Lay of the Werewolf,* a romance written in the thirteenth century by Marie de France, a Frenchwoman writing for the English court. Her story concerned a noble Breton household, whose mistress, a baroness, doubted her husband's fidelity; he disappeared three nights each week. When she questioned him, he revealed his secret. Because of a curse, he was doomed to spend those nights as a werewolf—*bisclaravet,* in the Breton dialect—and live by blood and violence. What gave him human form was clothing, he said: When he removed it, he became a wolf.

His revelations were incautious to say the least. Repelled, the baroness persuaded a knight of the court to steal her husband's clothes while he roamed abroad as an animal. This the gallant did, thus dooming the baron to perpetual roving in the forest.

Declaring herself widowed, the baroness married her accomplice and all might have gone well for both had not the king of Brittany been out hunting in the forest and come upon the werewolf. Cornered, torn by the dogs, the baron took a desperate chance. Grasping the king's stirrup in his paws, he licked his former master's boot. Amazed, the king took the unusual animal back to court, where he became the royal pet, treated respectfully by all. In his gratitude, the wolf exhibited model behavior.

But then the knight arrived at the castle. Usually docile, the werewolf recognized him as his betrayer and suddenly attacked, driving the knight away. The king and the wolf later visited the unfaithful baroness. Hurling himself on her, the wolf bit off her nose. After that, the truth was revealed. The baroness confessed to her crime, and she returned her husband's clothes, which restored him to his true form. For their betrayal, the baroness and her knight were driven into exile.

Europe's Lupine Terror

Europeans—especially those in isolated hamlets—for centuries lived with an omnipresent fear of wolves. Many documented accounts of encounters with the beasts show why. One such report from France details the 1783 attack on an eight-months-pregnant woman by a rabid wolf—which had already savaged a strong young man. Heavy with child the trembling woman found herself cornered by the snarling creature. In one powerful leap, the beast knocked her to the ground and sank its foaming jaws into her side.

Although the wolf was eventually hunted down and killed, the victim and her child—who was born prematurely because of the attack—died soon after. Such horrific tales were all too common in some regions of Europe; it is not surprising that the animal's name was attached to the demonic figure of the werewolf.

According to certain authorities, a healthy wolf will not attack a human being. They blame rabid wolves and dog-and-wolf hybrids for all the historic European attacks. War and famine in the Middle Ages also helped to secure the wolf's evil reputation, es-

The technique of driving wolves into nets hanging near carrion bait is illustrated in the Book of the Hunt, a treatise from the 1300s.

pecially in France. The creatures routinely fed on unprotected livestock and scavenged battlefield corpses. When made desperate by a shortage of normal prey, the animals braved greater threats. In the early 1400s, a fearsome pack, either wolves or crossbreeds, breached the gates of Paris, terrorizing women and children in the search for food. An even more ferocious pack, prowling fields near the city in 1439, savaged thirteen adults and children.

Small wonder, then, that throughout Europe the wolf retained its reputation as a savage predator, the object of fascination and loathing. And the low, mournful howling of a wolf in the night still can strike a chord of fear in all but the bravest of travelers.

A wolf falls prey to methods taught in the Book of the Hunt. By sixteenth-century French law, large-scale hunts were held three times a year to reduce the lupine population in every parish. The Book of the Hunt described the habits of wolves and all manner of ways to entrap, drive, shoot, and hound them.

Driven to a frenzy by hunger, a pack of wolves or dog-and-wolf hybrids swarms into a stockaded German village to attack a peasant family in this engraving from the sixteenth century.

As centuries passed, there arrived a point when fanciful stories told to amuse were replaced by real incidents and real suffering. Suddenly, tales such as Stubbe's started to emerge. It was as if people believed that werewolves were everywhere. The trial records on lycanthropy reveal an epidemic of cases. In France alone, between 1520 and 1630, some 30,000 individuals had the misfortune to be labeled werewolves; many of them underwent criminal investigation and torture, confessed, and suffered a vile death at the stake. For those who escaped such a fate, the trauma of interrogation must have left lifetime scars.

Among the first of the French werewolf trials to gain widespread notoriety was that of Pierre Burgot and Michel Verdun, two peasants who were tried in 1521. Burgot told a strange tale. Nineteen years earlier, he had been tending his flock of sheep when a violent storm broke out. As he ran about trying to collect the frightened animals, he came upon three horsemen, dressed in black, on black steeds. One of them asked him what was wrong, and the breathless Burgot told him that some of his sheep were lost and that he feared they would fall prey to wolves. The stranger said not to worry, that if Burgot would agree to serve him as his lord and master, he would protect the sheep in the days and years ahead and give him money as well. Accepting the proposition, Burgot agreed to meet again with the stranger, who called himself Moyset.

When the meeting took place, Moyset announced the full terms of the deal: Burgot must do nothing less than renounce God, the Holy Virgin, the Company of Heaven, his baptism, and his confirmation. Burgot accepted, swearing also never to assist at mass or to use holy water. Then he kissed Moyset's hand; it was as cold, he said, as the hand of a dead man.

As the years passed, Burgot weakened in his resolve to obey Moyset, and for this he was called to task by Michel Verdun, who demanded that he strip naked and let himself be anointed with a magic salve. The unguent soon had its effect, convincing Burgot that he had metamorphosed into a wolf. He was amazed to see his arms and legs grow hairy and his hands and feet become paws. Rubbing himself with the salve, Verdun also changed shape, and together they ran amuck through the surrounding countryside.

As werewolves, Burgot and Verdun committed a variety of gruesome crimes. They attacked a seven-year-old boy and tore him to pieces, killed a woman who was picking peas, and abducted a four-year-old girl and consumed all of her but her arm. Impelled by a growing cannibalistic appetite, they took to lapping up the blood of their victims. They even mated with female wolves.

The trial of Burgot and Verdun before Maitre Jean Bodin, the prior of a Dominican convent at Poligny in Franche-Comté, attracted large crowds. The so-called werewolves and their accomplice were convicted and duly put to death, and pictures of them were put up in the local church as a reminder to all of the evil deeds that men can commit under the influence of the devil.

Such warnings apparently had little effect. Lycanthropy trials only increased in

the years following. In 1573, for example, the depredations of an alleged werewolf, who had left several of his child victims half eaten, prompted the authorities of the town of Dôle in Franche-Comté province to issue an unusual edict: "According to the advertisement made to the Sovereign Court of Parliament at Dôle, that, in the territories of Espagny, Salvange, Courchapon, and the neighboring villages, has often been seen and met, for some time past, a werewolf, who, it is said, has already seized and carried off several little children, so that they have not been seen since, and since he has attacked and done injury in the country to some horsemen, who kept him off only with great difficulty and danger to their persons: the said Court, desiring to prevent any greater danger, has permitted, and does permit, those who are abiding or dwelling in the said places and others, notwithstanding all edicts concerning the chase and to pursue the said werewolf in every place where they may find or seize him: to tie and to kill, without incurring any pains or penalties." In other words, the town's leaders put a price on the werewolf's head.

Two months after the edict was issued, a man called Gilles Garnier, "the hermit of Dôle," was arrested as a werewolf; whether he was the one the vigilantes were hunting the record does not say. The document listing his crimes and sentencing him to death survives and is a litany of ghastly murders.

One typical paragraph of the document runs:

"It is proven that on a certain day, shortly after the Feast of St. Michael last, Gilles Garnier, being in the form of a wolf, seized upon in a vineyard a young girl, aged about ten or twelve years, and there he slew and killed her both with his hands, seemingly paws, as with his teeth, and having dragged the body with his hands and teeth into the aforesaid Bois de la Serre, he stripped her naked and not content with eating heartily of the flesh of her thighs and arms, he carried some of her flesh to Apolline his wife at the hermit-

Strung up on a gibbet, the body of the notorious Werewolf of Ansbach serves as a stern warning against evil in this engraving depicting the creature's capture and punishment. The beast, thought to be the incarnation of a recently deceased burgomaster, terrorized a Bavarian hamlet in 1685, preying on the flesh of women and children. Slain after falling into a well, the alleged werewolf was displayed wearing a mask, clothing, and a wig like the one affected by the late townsman.

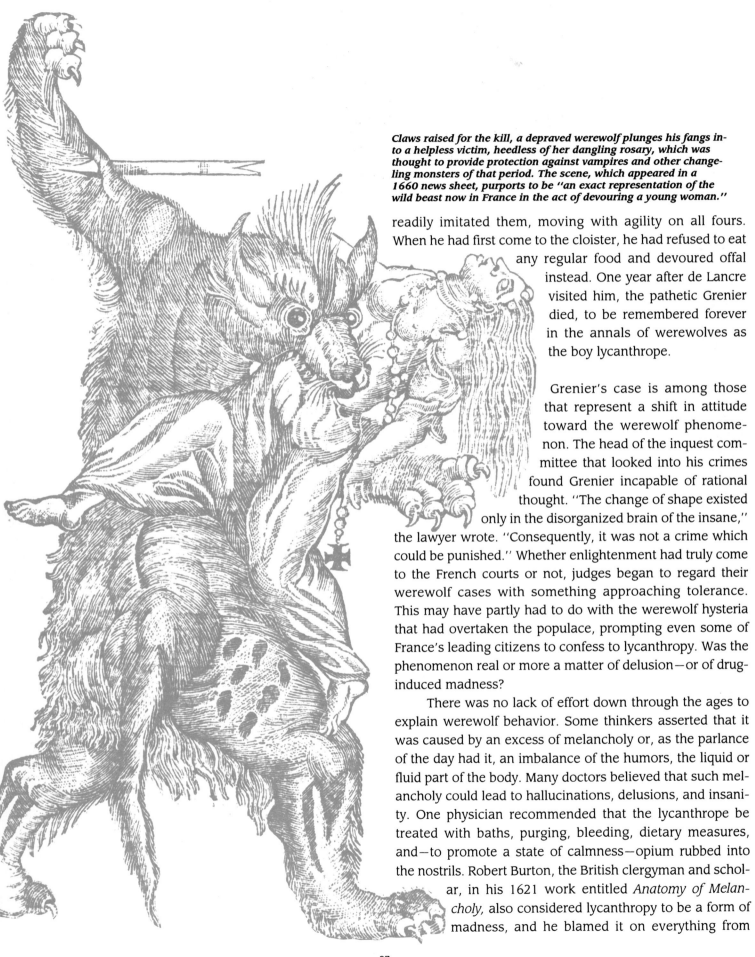

readily imitated them, moving with agility on all fours. When he had first come to the cloister, he had refused to eat any regular food and devoured offal instead. One year after de Lancre visited him, the pathetic Grenier died, to be remembered forever in the annals of werewolves as the boy lycanthrope.

Grenier's case is among those that represent a shift in attitude toward the werewolf phenomenon. The head of the inquest committee that looked into his crimes found Grenier incapable of rational thought. "The change of shape existed only in the disorganized brain of the insane," the lawyer wrote. "Consequently, it was not a crime which could be punished." Whether enlightenment had truly come to the French courts or not, judges began to regard their werewolf cases with something approaching tolerance. This may have partly had to do with the werewolf hysteria that had overtaken the populace, prompting even some of France's leading citizens to confess to lycanthropy. Was the phenomenon real or more a matter of delusion—or of drug-induced madness?

There was no lack of effort down through the ages to explain werewolf behavior. Some thinkers asserted that it was caused by an excess of melancholy or, as the parlance of the day had it, an imbalance of the humors, the liquid or fluid part of the body. Many doctors believed that such melancholy could lead to hallucinations, delusions, and insanity. One physician recommended that the lycanthrope be treated with baths, purging, bleeding, dietary measures, and—to promote a state of calmness—opium rubbed into the nostrils. Robert Burton, the British clergyman and scholar, in his 1621 work entitled *Anatomy of Melancholy*, also considered lycanthropy to be a form of madness, and he blamed it on everything from

Leaving a trail of mutilated corpses and severed limbs, a huge preda-
tor dubbed the Beast of Gevaudan wrought havoc in southeastern
France between 1764 and 1767, killing more than 100 people. The
slaying of a large wolf failed to halt the attacks, convincing peas-
ants that they faced something devilish, perhaps a werewolf able to
"charm" firearms and survive bullets. A special mass and the kill-
ing of a second wolf eventually brought a close to the reign of terror.

sorcerers and witches to poor diet, bad air, sleeplessness, and even lack of exercise.

However close such views came to the truth, they were not widely adopted. Instead, a frightened populace preferred magical explanations. Thus, for some, the were-wolf was the projection of a demon, who made its victim appear in his own eyes and to those around him as a wolf. For others, the werewolf was a direct manifestation of the devil. Early-seventeenth-century French author Henri Bouguet believed, as did a great many people of the day, that Satan would leave the lycanthrope asleep behind a bush, go forth as a wolf, and perform whatever evil might be in that person's mind. According to Bouguet, the devil could confuse the sleeper's imagination to such an extent "that he believes he has really been a wolf and has run about and killed men and beasts."

If wolves were a natural evil, comparable to plague or famine, werewolves apparently had to be considered a su-pernatural evil. Since the Bible offered no clue as to how the phenomenon should be regarded, it was up to theorists in the Church to rationalize it. This was by no means easy. To

say that Satan could indeed turn men and women into wolves would directly contradict one of the most important doctrines of Christianity—namely, that only God has the power to create. But then if sorcerers or demons could not create a wolf, could they transpose their souls into the already existing cor-puses of wolves? Again doctrine said no. Such a transformation would con-stitute an alteration of divine reality, implying that the shapeshifter, whether human or demon, had powers equiva-lent to God's.

Some, noting that the devil was a master of delusion, came up with a counter theory. "God alone can per-form real miracles," wrote Saint Thom-as Aquinas in his *Summa theologica,* "but the demons are permitted to perform lying wonders, extraordinary to us, and they employ certain seeds that exist in the elements of the world by which operation they seem to effect transfor-mations." Aquinas enumerated three ways in which such evil spirits might delude people: "by exhibiting as present what is not really there, by exhibiting what is there as other than it really is, and by concealing what is really there so that it appears as if it were not."

The argument would go on for centuries. Physicians more and more came to see the werewolf phenomenon as a manifestation of mental derangement. Other theorists an-alyzed it in terms of paranormal experience and the occult. In his book *The Mysteries of Magic,* the nineteenth-century French occultist Éliphas Lévi dismissed the "furious mani-as" that medicine ascribed to lycanthropes and, instead, postulated the existence of a sidereal, or phantom, body that acted as mediator between the soul and a material or-ganism. "Thus in the case of a man whose instinct is sav-age and sanguinary, his phantom will wander abroad in lu-pine form, whilst he sleeps painfully at home, dreaming he is a veritable wolf.'' Lévi believed that the wound doubling, so often reported in the cases of werewolves, could be attributed to the out-of-body experience. He saw the human body as subject to magnetic as well as nervous influences and, he thought that through these means, it was capable of receiving the wounds suffered by the transformed shape.

At the turn of the century, those students of the paranormal, the Theosophists, proposed their own theories. A principal leader of the movement,

An 1806 work on physiognomy—the reading of character traits based on physical features—contended that appearance could indicate inherent lycanthropy.

Charles Webster Leadbeater, considered wound doubling to be the product of a person's astral projection receiving a wound and that wound transferring to the material body through a complicated process called repercussion. As for the origin of werewolves, Leadbeater was convinced that entities in an astral existence can materialize the astral body of a person inclined to violence and brutality and control it, reshaping it into a wolf or other fierce animal and propelling it on its evil course.

Known to the French as me-
neurs de loup, or wolf charmers, men like the shadowy piper
in this nineteenth-century litho-
graph were said to befriend
wolves and live among them.
Usually hermits, itinerant pip-
ers, and others on the fringes of
peasant society, wolf charmers
reportedly commanded their
lupine comrades, leading them
in frightful, howling song.

The finer points continue to be argued among occultists and others even to this day. Rose Gladden, a British exorcist and clairvoyant, thinks astral projection may be behind the activities of werewolves. "Suppose I was a cruel person," she says, "who enjoyed the horrible things in life. Well, as I projected my astral body out of my physical body, all the surrounding evil could grasp me. And it would be the evil grasping my astral projection, or grasping my 'double,' which would transform me into an animal or wolf. Evil forces find it much easier to exist within mankind—within an evil man, say—than in a nebulous vacuum. People addicted to werewolfery were—indeed, still are the most evil manifestations of humanity."

That many people believe that werewolves still exist is more than borne out by the response to Fox Broadcasting's Werewolf Hotline. There are even individuals today who believe they are werewolves, and some of these lycanthropes have been studied and treated by psychologists and psychiatrists. The November 1975 issue of *The Canadian Psychiatric Association Journal,* noting that this "allegedly extinct condition" had been omitted from most contemporary medical textbooks, reported in detail on several recent cases of lycanthropy.

In the first case, the twenty-year-old patient, referred to as Mr. H, was convinced that he was a werewolf. A drug user, he told his doctor that while serving in the United States Army in Europe, he had hiked into a forest near his post and had ingested LSD and strychnine, the latter a deadly poison that acts as a stimulant when taken in tiny quantities. Both substances are pharmacologically similar to some of the ingredients used by shapeshifters in the past. They had an instant and potent effect on the young man, who claimed to have seen fur growing on his hands and felt it sprouting on his face. Soon he was overcome by a compulsion to chase after, catch, and devour live rabbits. He wandered in this delusional state for several days before returning to the post.

Placed on the tranquilizer chlorpromazine, Mr. H was weaned away from drugs and received adjunct therapy for some nine months, during which time he continued to hear disembodied voices and to experience satanic visions. Claiming to be possessed by the devil, he insisted he had unusual powers. Tests indicated his delusions were "compatible with acute schizophrenic or toxic psychosis." He was treated with an antipsychotic drug, and when he improved sufficiently, he was referred to an outpatient clinic. After only two visits, however, he had stopped taking the medication and left treatment. Subsequent efforts to contact him failed.

Another werewolf patient, thirty-seven-year-old Mr. W was admitted to the hospital after repeated public displays of bizarre activity, including howling at the moon, sleeping in cemeteries, allowing his hair and beard to grow out, and lying in the center of busy highways. Unlike Mr. H, Mr. W had no history of drug or alcohol abuse. He had once been a farmer and considered of average intelligence, as an IQ test administered when he served in the United States Navy had indicated. Now, he was seen not only as psychotic but also as intellectually deficient, with a mental age of an eight- to ten-year-old child.

Because of the patient's increasing dementia, the doctors performed a brain biopsy. Their findings revealed an abnormal physiological deterioration of cerebral tissue, known as walnut brain. Mr. W was diagnosed as having a chronic brain syndrome of unknown origin. When placed on antipsychotic drugs, he showed no further symptoms of lycanthropy. Seen later on an outpatient basis, he exhibited quiet, childlike behavior.

The October 1977 issue of *The American Journal of Psychiatry* details the particularly bizarre story of a forty-nine-year-old woman who believed herself a wolf and, with increasing frequency, had begun acting like one. She revealed that just below the surface of a seemingly normal twenty-year marriage she had harbored a consuming desire to indulge in secret, bestial appetites. Her erotic daydreams often involved other women in polymorphous perverse

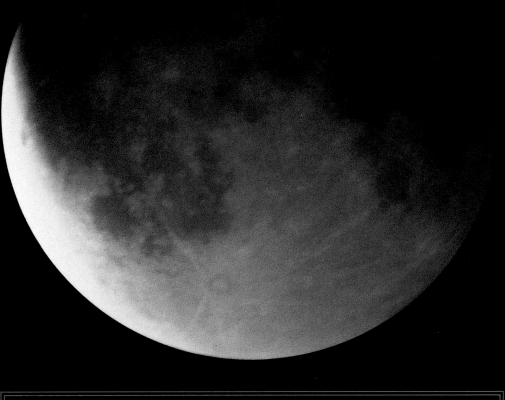

The Bright Moon's Dark Power

As keeper of the night, the moon has been accorded a baneful role in earthly affairs. Wolves howl at it, robbers are guided by its light, vampires and werewolves are reputed to revel in its glow. Virtually every sort of misfortune has been attributed to the moon's influence—alcoholism, suicide, murder, arson, birth defects, and mental illness. (The word *lunacy* comes from the Latin for moon, *luna*.)

Science has been enlisted to aid our understanding of the satellite's force. A Duke University professor has asserted that changes in the brain's electrical activity coincide with lunar phases. Other studies connect the moon to increases in strokes and epileptic seizures. The researchers claim that

drugs have greater effect, enzymes and hormones are more active, and the body's metabolism increases during the full moon. Using less formal methods, police often note that especially violent crimes often occur during periods of full moon. The nationwide murder rate, for instance, has been alleged to jump 50 percent during a full moon, while in New York City, the incidence of arson has been said to double.

Many scientists reject this so-called moon madness. They say that only the ocean tides owe their action to the moon and that any other events attributed to it can be blamed on coincidence, faulty scientific methods, or error. Still, research into lunar effects continues, a search for the orb's enigmatic power.

orgies. The wolf was a constant and central figure in her fantasies; she felt its mesmerizing stare fastened onto her by day, its hot breath on her bare neck at night. Soon she began "feeling like an animal with claws." For her, the message was clear—she was a wolf.

After a time, she began to act out her compulsions. At a family gathering, for instance, she was suddenly overwhelmed by the wolf passion. Stripping naked and dropping to all fours she excitedly approached her own mother, and assuming the sexual posture of a female wolf, she offered herself. The woman's state continued to deteriorate; the next evening, after making love to her husband, she lapsed into a frenetic two-hour episode of grunting and of clawing and gnawing at the bed. She explained afterward that the devil "came into her body and she became an animal."

Enrolled in an inpatient program, she received daily psychotherapy and was placed on medication. In the first three weeks she suffered relapses, during which she would rave: "I am a wolf of the night, I am wolf woman of the day. . . . I have claws, teeth, fangs, hair . . . and anguish is my prey at night . . . powerless is my cause. I am what I am and will always roam the earth after death. . . . I will continue to search for perfection and salvation." Concurrently she experienced the urge to kill accompanied by a consuming sexual excitement.

She now saw the head of a wolf, rather than her own face, when she gazed in the mirror. The medical staff commented on "the unintelligible, animal-like noises she made." There was some improvement, but the patient then relapsed during the full moon. Writing about her experience, she stated: "I don't intend to give up the search for (what) I lack . . . in my present marriage . . . my search for such a hairy creature. I will haunt the graveyards for a tall, dark man that I intend to find." After nine weeks of treatment, she was released from the hospital on a regimen of drugs designed to free her of her delusion.

On the basis of the woman's symptoms, her doctors were able to formulate a psychological profile of the ly-

canthrope, which is not so different, in spite of its modern medical language, from the conclusions of some of the more enlightened physicians and thinkers of earlier times. They saw the lycanthrope as suffering from "(1) schizophrenia, (2) organic brain syndrome with psychosis, (3) psychotic depressive reaction, (4) hysterical neurosis of the dissociative type, (5) manic-depressive psychosis, and (6) psychomotor epilepsy."

Although such symptoms seem to apply to many of the cases of lycanthropy recorded over the years, they do not cover all. The haunting image of the werewolf—with his red eyes, red nails, hairy body, and scabrous skin—is yet to be explained. And something else must be considered as well: the distinct possibility that some so-called werewolves were in fact the tragic victims of rabies. A strain of virus carried by dogs, wolves, and other mammals, including vampire bats in the New World, the disease strikes the central nervous system. In humans it elicits uncontrollable excitement and produces painful contractions of the throat muscles, which prevent the victim from drinking. Without medical intervention, death usually occurs within three to five days of the first symptoms.

Records from the past suggest the occasional presence of rabies in medieval Europe. An edict of the archbishop of York, dating from 766, states: "If a wolf shall attack cattle of any kind, and the animal so attacked shall thereof die, no Christian may eat of it." Whether this measure was designed to guard against lycanthropy or rabies is not exactly clear, but it seems a wise admonishment in light of an occurrence four hundred years later in which a presumably rabid wolf bit "two and twenty persons, all of whom in a short space died."

Another physical condition that may have been mistaken for lycanthropy is porphyria, a rare genetic disorder that results in a deficiency of heme, one of the pigments in the oxygen-carrying red blood cells. At the 1985 conference of the American Association for the Advancement of Science, biochemist David Dolphin suggested that the untreated symptoms of porphyria match many of the traits as-

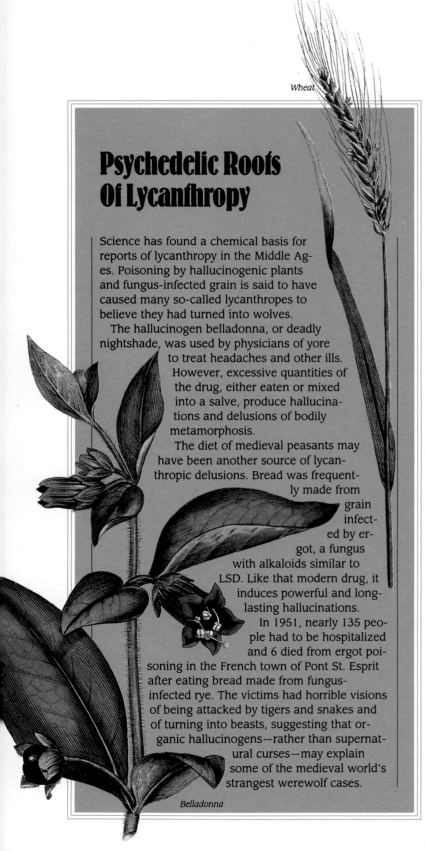

Wheat

Psychedelic Roots Of Lycanthropy

Science has found a chemical basis for reports of lycanthropy in the Middle Ages. Poisoning by hallucinogenic plants and fungus-infected grain is said to have caused many so-called lycanthropes to believe they had turned into wolves.

The hallucinogen belladonna, or deadly nightshade, was used by physicians of yore to treat headaches and other ills. However, excessive quantities of the drug, either eaten or mixed into a salve, produce hallucinations and delusions of bodily metamorphosis.

The diet of medieval peasants may have been another source of lycanthropic delusions. Bread was frequently made from grain infected by ergot, a fungus with alkaloids similar to LSD. Like that modern drug, it induces powerful and long-lasting hallucinations.

In 1951, nearly 135 people had to be hospitalized and 6 died from ergot poisoning in the French town of Pont St. Esprit after eating bread made from fungus-infected rye. The victims had horrible visions of being attacked by tigers and snakes and of turning into beasts, suggesting that organic hallucinogens—rather than supernatural curses—may explain some of the medieval world's strangest werewolf cases.

Belladonna

sociated with the classic lycanthrope. One of these is severe photosensitivity, which makes venturing out into daylight extremely painful and thus relegates the sufferer to a life of shadows and darkness. Moreover, as the condition advances, the victim's appearance grows increasingly morbid. Discoloration of the skin and hypertrichosis, an unusual and thick growth of facial or body hair, can develop. There is a tendency for skin lesions to form and ulcerate, eventually attacking cartilage and bone and causing a progressive deterioration of the nose, ears, eyelids, and fingers. And the teeth, as well as the fingernails and the flesh beneath them, might turn red or reddish brown because of deposition of porphyrin, a component of hemoglobin in the blood. The disease is often accompanied by mental disturbances, running the gamut from mild hysteria to delirium and manic-depressive psychoses.

Porphyria may have cropped up in certain areas where the gene pool was restricted, and because the disease is an inherited condition, the cases of lycanthropy would therefore be more numerous in some regions than in others. During a period when the general understanding of medical conditions was at best imperfect, the pathetically transformed sufferer could easily become an outcast as well as a scapegoat, with his or her condition ascribed to demonic influences.

Although rabies, porphyria, drug use, and psychosis may largely explain the werewolf phenomenon, the willingness of so many people over the centuries to believe in a creature so far outside the bounds of reality suggests that lycanthropy struck chords deep within the human psyche. Today, now that the wolves have long ceased to be a threat, it may be hard for us to understand our ancestors' fears and secret wishes that bound them to the beast. Indeed now that we have the power to devastate the earth many times over, the ferocious strength of the wolf seems puny by comparison. Yet perhaps the essence of the myths and seeds of demonic delusion have nothing to do with real wolves. Perhaps they have something to say about the shadow wolf that may be lurking in us all.

Ritual for an Evil Change

Hail, hail, hail, great Wolf Spirit, hail! / A boon I ask thee, mighty shade, / Within this circle I have made. / Make me a werewolf strong and bold, / The terror alike of young and old." Thus begins an ancient incantation, at one time part of the werewolf transformation ritual presented in an artist's reconstruction on the following pages. The lycanthropic literature of the past is filled with such eerie chants, delivered in desolate locations, sometimes from within the perimeters of mysterious circles scratched onto the ground, and generally beneath the ghostly light of a full moon.

As invocations of evil, the chants called upon the spirits of the "earthbound dead, that glide with noiseless tread," the spirits of the trees and air, of heat and fire, of cold and ice. Repeating the chants over and over again, the votary prepared himself psychically for his experience. Yet however intently he might feel the words, they were not enough to bring him to the altered state of mind that would enable him to kill and eat his victims. Essential was a girdle or belt cut from the skin of a wolf or a hanged murderer, to be worn around the waist. But more important by far were the vapors that he might inhale or the salves or ointments with which he rubbed his naked body. Made from ingredients as foul as they were potent, these contained psychoactive substances that released the beast within the lycanthrope and set him on his bloody course, in the company, as one chant has it, of the "elect of all the devilish hosts—wolves, vampires, satyrs, ghosts!"

With evil intent, a man traces two circles in flat ground according to an age-old formula. When he has completed the second circle, he will build a fire of pine or larch and black poplar, then will suspend an iron cauldron from the tripod. Into this he will drop four or five of the following ingredients: opium, poppy seeds, aloe, henbane, hemlock, parsley, solanine (an extract of nightshade) and asafetida, a gum resin. After stirring all the components together in the cauldron, he will start the fire and allow the contents to simmer. When the flames leap up, he will begin his incantation: "Elect of all devilish hosts, I pray you send hither, the great gray shape that makes men shiver. Come! Come! Come!"

Having removed his clothing and put on a wolf-skin girdle, the initiate now rubs his entire body with a hallucinogenic salve. Such ointments, which were absorbed through the skin, were made from ingredients as varied as camphor, aconite, aniseed, opium, poplar leaves, bat's blood, and soot, mixed with the rendered fat of a cat. Before the ointment begins to take effect, the man breathes in the intoxicating fumes floating from the bubbling cauldron, which prepare him mentally for the next stage of this strange ritual.

Under the double influence of the fumes and salve, the man falls to his knees, imploring the spirit of the unknown to bestow on him the power of metamorphosis. With his hands raised, he intones these words: "I beg, I pray, I implore thee —thee unparalleled Phantom of Darkness—to make me a werewolf . . . *a werewolf!*" Within the man's hallucinogen-charged mind, a malevolent form has already begun to reveal itself. He feels as if his own body is changing, growing hairier, his nails lengthening into claws. His words resound into the night: "Make me a man-eater. Make me a woman-eater. Make me a child-eater. Make me a werewolf!"

Fully transformed, at least in his own mind, the werewolf bounds off into the darkness. Having vowed "heart, body, and soul" to serve the powers of evil, he is fated now to wander each day between sunset and sunup in search of human flesh. But however strong and menacing he thinks himself, he knows that even as a werewolf he will be vulnerable, hence he must chant as a charm the final words of the transformation ceremony: "Melt the bullet, blunt the knife, rot the cudgel, strike fear into man, beast, and reptile so they may not seize the gray wolf, nor tear him from his warm hide. My word is firm, firmer than sleep or the strength of heroes."

Transylvania's Real-Life Dracula

Dracula. For millions, the name evokes the sinister vampire from the darkly mysterious land of Transylvania, the famous fictional corpse-by-day, killer-by-night who has sent shudders through generations of readers and moviegoers since 1897, when he appeared as the title character of Bram Stoker's great horror novel. What fewer people realize is that the name of Stoker's immortal character was taken from a real Dracula who lived in the real Transylvania four centuries earlier. And although that original Dracula was not a bloodsucking vampire, he was a cruel tyrant whose appalling brutalities make his fictional namesake seem by comparison an almost amiable fellow.

The real-life Dracula was born in 1430 or 1431 in the old Transylvanian town of Sighişoara. He was the second son of Vlad II, prince of Walachia, and when he eventually succeeded his father he was titled Vlad III, although he became better known as Vlad Tepes, or Vlad the Impaler. His father was called Dracul, "the devil," perhaps because he was a fearsome warrior or possibly because he was a member of a Catholic organization of knights called the Order of the Dragon and in those parts a dragon was the devil's symbol. In any case, Vlad III called himself Dracula, "son of Dracul."

Dracula was a fierce warrior, but it was sometimes difficult to know whose side he was on in the interminable struggle between eastern and western empires, churches, and cultures that wracked his land. He shifted allegiances as he willed, from Turkish overlords to Hungarians, from the Roman Catholic church to Orthodoxy, even serving Islamic causes when he was allied with the Ottomans. In the political chaos of the time and place, his hold on power was never secure: On three occasions, he ruled and lost Walachia, a southern Rumanian principality that included parts of Transylvania.

Dracula was first placed on the Walachian throne in 1448 by the Turks, after his father and older brother had been assassinated by the Hungarian governor's agents. Fearful of the Turks who sponsored him, he fled but returned to the

This woodcut from the title page of a 1493 German pamphlet is believed to be an accurate portrait of Vlad the Impaler, the actual Dracula—and it resembles Bram Stoker's description of his fictional Dracula.

throne in 1456 with Hungarian support.

It was during the next six years, his longest reign, that his reputation for spectacular cruelty began to grow. The torture and execution of political opponents were not unusual in the fourteenth and fifteenth centuries: This was a violent, war-torn age dominated by tyrants. But Vlad's atrocities—said to have been used later as models by Ivan the Terrible of Russia—were remarkable even in this era. It was not the number of Vlad's murders that horrified people, it was the sadistic nature of the murders they abhorred. According to one account, he ambushed a group of Turks with whom he had arranged a truce meeting. In an action tantamount to a declaration of war, he took them to his capital city, Tîrgovişte, where he stripped them and impaled them on spikes.

His victims came to include not only the enemy but his own people—nobles and peasants—and hapless travelers. Apparently because he believed they were spies, he once rounded up and impaled a number of merchants who were passing through his country on holiday—and democratically impaled some of their carriage drivers as well. On another occasion and for similar reasons, he called together some 400 foreign students, mainly boys, who were in Walachia to learn the language and customs, assembled them in one room, then had the building burned down.

His typical impalement victim was hoisted on a stake thrust through the rectum. But Dracula added variations as he made a specialty, even a sadistic art form, of impaling. He impaled people from the front, back, and side; through the stomach, breast, navel, and groin. He had them impaled from above, while they hung upside down, and with rounded-off stakes, to prolong the torture.

He devised various forms of impalement for people of different ages, sex, and rank and had the stakes arranged in geometric patterns and at different heights. For reasons unknown, he is reported to have impaled the entire population of a village in concentric circles on a hillside, putting the town officials at the top where they had one last look down from their accustomed position. He added embellishments, driving nails through heads, cutting off limbs, noses, ears, and

sex organs, and dabbling in strangulation, burning, boiling in oil, and blinding. He seemed to take great pleasure in his foul deeds, especially when his impaled victims, as one report put it, "twisted around and twitched like frogs." On viewing such a performance he would often say: "Oh, what great gracefulness they exhibit!"

Thanks in part to the recent invention

Mounted on a rearing charger and raising his sword high, Dracula is ready to do heroic battle against the Turks in this Rumanian portrait, a naive painting on glass.

of the printing press, stories of Dracula's heinous deeds spread across Europe during his life and after. He was a favorite subject for the new printed handbills and pamphlets that were circulating among the literate classes. Presaging the kind of magazine-cover billings that would be seen on newsstands five hundred years later, the title page of a typical German publication carried a taste of the horror readers would find within: "The shocking story of a MONSTER and BERSERKER called Dracula who committed such un-christian deeds as killing men by placing them on stakes, hacking them to pieces

like cabbage, boiling mothers and children alive and compelling men to acts of cannibalism." The public relished such macabre accounts, guaranteeing big sales. Thus Dracula became, in effect, perhaps the first true international celebrity created by the mass media.

Despite his misdeeds in his homeland, Vlad was and remains in Rumanian lore a heroic figure who fought off invaders. Elsewhere, his reputation was one of unalloyed notoriety. German publications, especially, concentrated on his most gruesome behavior, since he ruthlessly massacred Transylvanians of German extraction. But enough awful details of his acts have been confirmed from other sources—Russian accounts, the memoirs of Pope Pius II (whose legate in Hungary met Dracula), and Rumanian folk ballads—to indicate that the German pamphlets cannot be dismissed as mere propaganda.

One of Dracula's most notorious atrocities chronicled by the pamphlets occurred on April 2, 1459, in the city of Braşov as the result of his longstanding dispute with merchants of the region. At daybreak, his troops began herding the townspeople to a knoll below a chapel at the edge of town. There were at least 20,000 of them, by most counts—men and women, children and the elderly. They watched in terror as the invaders burned their homes. Then came Dracula's traditional order: impalement. By day's end, the hillside was a forest of stakes and the ground a stream of blood, as those who were not impaled had their heads chopped off.

During the slaughter, a local boyar, or noble, reportedly complained of the smell from blood and corpses. Exercising his perverted sense of humor, Dracula ordered the man to be impaled on a stake taller than the others so he would not be bothered by the stench. Dracula himself suffered no such queasiness. The account said he ate a hearty meal beneath the dying villagers.

Dracula could never be accused of showing favor to rank. On one occasion, he summoned the great boyars of the land and began to question them about how many different reigns they had seen. "Seven," "twenty," "thirty," the aristocrats boasted. They did not realize that Dracula wanted to avenge the brutal slayings of his father and brother and was

Dracula's soldiers descend on an assembly of dining nobles, or boyars, and drag them off to their deaths. Having invited the boyars to his palace for a great feast, possibly Easter, Dracula then ordered the impalement of some 500 of them. He spared the younger, most able-bodied nobles, however, so they could be used as slave labor to build a castle.

trying to determine which of the boyars had been around when their deaths occurred. Eventually, he had some 500 of them impaled near the palace.

Another time, it was a group of poor and old people whom Dracula invited to his palace. He passed out clothing and served them dinner. Then, while the guests relaxed, their host ordered the doors to be locked and the palace set on fire. "I have done this so that there should be no more poor in my land and so that they should no longer suffer in this world," Dracula reportedly explained.

Women were a special target. A well-known story tells of Dracula's meeting a peasant who was poorly dressed. "Your wife is assuredly the kind who remains idle," said the prince. "She is not worthy of living in my realm." Although the peasant protested that he was satisfied, Dracula had her impaled and found a new mate for the widower. Unfaithful wives, young women who lost their virginity, and unchaste widows reputedly could

expect harsher punishments. Their sex organs were cut, after which they were skinned alive and exhibited in public.

One story says that even Dracula's mistress was not spared. Finding him in a foul mood one day, she tried to cheer him up by telling him she was pregnant. Dracula accused her of lying; to prove it, he took out his sword and slit open her stomach. The account does not record whether he proved she was lying or not.

Dracula's vanity and temper showed up again when ambassadors from the Turkish sultan came to pay homage but did not take off their turbans when they bowed. Dracula demanded to know why they dishonored him in that way. "This is the custom with rulers of our country," they replied. Saying he would like to strengthen the custom, Dracula ordered the turbans nailed to their heads.

No one is certain how many were impaled, beheaded, roasted, and otherwise killed, tortured, or brutalized by Dracula. A papal legate, the bishop of Erlau, who

had no reason to exaggerate, reported a year before the tyrant's death that Dracula had authorized the killing of 100,000 people. But a survey of other accounts indicates that estimate may be too small.

Dracula lost his throne when the boyars deserted him in 1462, and he spent the next twelve years imprisoned in a Hungarian fortress. He was freed to fight the Ottomans, and in 1476, he ascended Walachia's throne yet again. A few weeks later, he fought his final battle, confronting a Turkish army outside Bucharest.

Accounts of his death vary. One suggests he was killed by treacherous boyars. Another says he was cut off from his men and, to avoid capture, disguised himself as a Turk. The plan misfired when his followers mistakenly killed him. However he died, his head was taken to the Turkish sultan in Constantinople. There, the head of Vlad the Impaler, the real Dracula, was impaled on a stake.

In a display of evil that would shock as well as titillate the European public (who would eagerly buy reproductions of the event such as this sixteenth-century German print), Vlad Tepes dines outside Brașov, his appetite undisturbed by the massacre being carried out at his order.

Vampires

Serbian peasant named Peter Plogojowitz died in 1725 and was buried in his village of Kisilova. A little more than two months later, nine other villagers, young and old, died within a single week. On their death beds, all of them claimed that Plogojowitz had come to them in their sleep, lain down upon them, and throttled the very life out of them—that Plogojowitz, instead of resting peacefully in his grave, had become a vampire. Plogojowitz's wife further terrified the frightened villagers when she told them that her dead husband had appeared to her and demanded his shoes. Then she fled Kisilova for another community.

At the time of the mysterious deaths, this part of Serbia was under Austria's imperial rule. Many Austrian bureaucrats had come to the region to administer its government, and one such official was asked by the Kisilova villagers to witness the opening of Plogojowitz's grave to look for signs that the peasant had become a bloodthirsty vampire.

Although the imperial provisor of the Gradisk District disapproved of the plans to disturb Plogojowitz's grave, the distraught villagers would not be dissuaded. They told the provisor that if they were not permitted to examine Plogojowitz's body and deal with it in time-honored fashion, they would abandon the village before they all were destroyed by the evil spirit. So the reluctant bureaucrat, with the Gradisk priest in tow, attended the opening of Plogojowitz's grave and reported that he observed what the peasants had feared: "The body, except for the nose, which was somewhat fallen away, was completely fresh," he wrote. "The hair and beard—even the nails, of which the old ones had fallen away—had grown on him; the old skin, which was somewhat whitish, had peeled away, and a new fresh one had emerged under it. . . . Not without astonishment, I saw some fresh blood in his mouth, which according to the common observation, he had sucked from the people killed by him."

These details revealing that the corpse had not started to decay were folklore "proof" that the body was that of a vampire. Beside themselves with fear, the villagers quickly sharpened a wooden stake and pierced Plogojowitz through the heart, which caused fresh blood to flow from his chest, his ears, and his mouth. Then the body was burned to ashes.

Plogojowitz lived and died in an era that saw a virtual plague of reported vampirism sweep through eastern Europe. During the seventeenth and eighteenth centuries, it was widely believed in that part of the world that the dead could be transformed into undead souls who preyed upon the living and could be warded off and killed only by certain methods. But the idea of these creatures and their horrifying appetite for blood was not unique to those centuries or that place. It had haunted the minds of humankind long before Plogojowitz's time—and would continue to do so thereafter. As recently as 1912, a Hungarian farmer became convinced that a fourteen-year-old boy who had died while in his employ was visiting him every night. According to a report at the time in London's *Daily Telegraph,* the frightened farmer and some friends dug up the boy's body, stuffed three pieces of garlic and three stones into its mouth, then fixed it to the ground with a stake driven through its chest. They told police they did this in order to stop the dead lad's threatening nocturnal visits.

Such fears still survive, lurking in some dark corner of the modern psyche, as witness their recurrent appearances in literature and films. The strong erotic element inherent in stories of vampires—who arrive under cover of night to suck the exposed necks of victims prostrate with fear and desire—may help to explain the popular fascination with such tales, particularly when they have been romanticized for the screen.

But despite the classic image of Count Dracula, the character created by novelist Bram Stoker that has become the model for most of the movie representations of the undead, not all vampires arise from coffins to feed upon the living nor transform themselves into bats to get from place to place. (The bat form, in fact, seems to have been Stoker's invention. Before his time, folklore had vampires transforming into many animal forms, but apparently not that of bats.) There are also real, living people who are considered or who consider themselves to be vampires, and who torture or kill unwary victims in a quest for blood. Whatever form vampirism takes, its hold upon the human imagination has endured for centuries.

From earliest times, people have believed that the soul lives on long after a person dies and in some cases retains enough power to reactivate the body. Therefore, ancient cultures took steps when preparing the dead for burial to make it difficult for the corpse to escape the grave and to propitiate departed souls so they would not want to come back to haunt the living. To placate the dead, survivors buried food, drink, and concubines beside them. But the living feared that the most urgent need likely to drive corpses from their coffins was a thirst for fresh, revitalizing blood.

It was this fear, apparently, that inspired ancient tales

of vampirelike creatures. Among the earliest was the Babylonians' *edimmu*. A troubled soul that could not rest, the edimmu wandered the earth searching for victims, whose veins it sucked. The Babylonians also took care not to offend the demon Lilitu, who was called Lilith by the ancient Hebrews. Legend held that Lilith was the first wife of Adam but was banished from the Garden of Eden after refusing to obey him. She became a demon who swept down to drink the blood of helpless infants and children. Lilith was also blamed for the erotic dreams of men, events that were regarded with horror because of the loss of semen.

Early Chinese feared the *qiang shi,* a demon that inhabited a corpse and prevented it from decaying by ingesting the blood of other corpses and living people. The appearance of the qiang shi, with its glaring eyes, sharp claws, and body covered with white or greenish hair, made it an especially potent horror. The Chinese further believed that an evil human soul needed only a skeleton or in some cases no more than a skull in order to become a vampire. They took precautions to ensure that cats were never allowed in the same room with corpses, for it was thought that if a cat jumped over a dead body it might impart its tiger nature to the corpse, which then surely would become a vampire. And if the sun or moon were allowed to shine on a corpse, the soul might be strengthened by the light and go forth to keep the body supplied with human blood to stave off decay.

The ancient Greeks talked of the *empusa,* a demonic

spirit that could enter a body. A similar demon was the lamia, a beautiful woman who embraced young men with the intention of drinking their blood. The word *lamia* was also used to describe grotesque women whose lower bodies were shaped like animals, often scaly serpents. That kind of lamia fed on flesh and flew about looking for the fresh blood of children.

The Arabs believed in the ghoul, a female demon familiar from *The Thousand and One Nights*—a collection of stories dating from sometime in the first millennium—who wandered cemeteries to feast upon the blood of the dead in their graves. She also plagued the living, lying in wait in secluded areas or in latrines to pounce upon travelers and drink their blood.

The advent of Christianity seemed to strengthen belief in the notion of the undead rising from their graves. Some early Christian writers mixed ancient pagan myths with Church doctrine about purgatory to tell of excommunicated people leaving their graves because their souls could find no peace. The Church's teachings of the mystical transubstantiation of Christ's body and blood, which were consumed by worshipers at mass, also reinforced the widely held belief in the regenerative power of blood. As Christianity spread throughout Europe, tales of vampire attacks became more frequent. A church-sanctioned book called the *Malleus Maleficarum,* or Hammer of Witches, first printed in 1486, described approved procedures for identifying and punishing vampires and other supernatural beings. Vampires were to be disinterred and decapitated.

Such folktales permeated the folklore of many early cultures around the world. But reports of vampires fairly similar to the ones we think of today first appeared in the sixteenth century in the Slavic regions of eastern Europe, in lands now situated in Hungary and Rumania. In 1526, Turkey's Süleyman the Magnificent defeated the Hungarian king in battle. Hungary was then divided into three parts, one ruled by the Turks, one by the Austrian Hapsburgs, and the other, an independent state called Transylvania, ruled by various local lords. In these remote, strife-torn regions the vampire superstition took firm root and flourished.

Transylvania, a remote land where armies fought mightily and nobles built gloomy castles upon the craggy slopes of the Carpathian Mountain foothills, has always seemed a mysterious place. The heavily forested country was at that time inhabited by superstitious peasants who believed that the soul, an entity distinct from the body, could leave the body, even during life, and travel about the world as a bird or as some other animal. A character in Bram Stoker's novel *Dracula* explains some of the reasons for the richness of the area's folklore: "In the population of Transylvania there are four distinct nationalities. Saxons in the south and, mixed with them, the Walachs (Rumanians), who are descendants of Dacians; Magyars in the west and Szekelys in the west and north. I read that every known superstition in the world is gathered into the horseshoe of the Carpathians, as if it were the centre of some sort of imaginative whirlpool."

Life at the center of the whirlpool was often a very real nightmare for Transylvanian peasants who eked out a living from the soil. Anywhere in southeastern Europe sudden plagues could depopulate whole towns. Such events enforced the belief in vampires, which were often blamed for the deaths. The tales that circulated stressed the predators' abominable stench, and the smell of vampires was thought to herald the coming of a plague.

Helpless in the face of an epidemic, terrified people buried the stricken immediately after they died—sometimes, accidentally, even before they had died, perhaps while the supposed corpses were in a comalike state called catalepsy, during which breathing may stop. Occasionally such unfortunate victims would awaken in their graves and attempt to claw their way out. Later,

As late as the 1800s, women in childbirth wore amulets such as this one from Persia to protect their babies from the bloodsucking demon Lilith, depicted here as an owl. Legend held that Lilith would spare children after reading the sacred inscriptions on the amulet.

A fanged mask with a fiery tongue symbolizes the vampirelike Rangda, a Balinese demon thought to leave its victims stiff limbed, drooling, and demented.

grave robbers, or fellow peasants alarmed by some clue that the deceased were vampires, would dig them up and discover their bodies twisted and tortured from efforts to escape suffocation.

Considering the state of medical knowledge, it was easy for those who opened a grave and found blood beneath the fingernails of a corpse or a mouth agape in an eternal scream to conclude that yet another vampire had been discovered. Of course, if a mistakenly buried person were disinterred before dying and actually sat up or otherwise displayed signs of life when the coffin was opened, the indications of vampirism were even more dramatically evident, and a stake driven through the chest would unfortunately put that body permanently to rest too.

Although it was believed that anyone with fresh red blood in his veins could fall victim to a vampire—and thus himself become one, since that bite conveyed the condition as surely as a rabid dog's bite spread hydrophobia—European folklore held that certain types of people were more likely to be transformed into vampires than others. Society's outcasts, always viewed with suspicion, were considered likely to return from the grave. So were redheads, people born with cauls, breech babies, children born on Christmas Day—

and just about anyone who was born under unusual circumstances or whose appearance was somehow strange or whose behavior was different from the norm. Those with cleft palates were particularly suspect, since the deformity caused a drawing up of the lip. In Greece, where most people had dark eyes, those with blue eyes were considered likely vampires. Suicides were prime candidates to rise again as vampires, as were those who had died after being excommunicated from the Church. The Greek Orthodox church held that the body of someone who had been excommunicated did not decay after death unless the corpse had been granted absolution (in contrast to the Roman church, whose doctrines held that God preserved only saintly corpses from decay).

So strong was the Greek belief in vampires, called *vrykolkas,* that in the nineteenth century, bodies were dug up after three years to make sure they had turned to bones and dust. Greeks believed vrykolkas were not really the souls of the deceased but evil spirits that entered the body after the soul had withdrawn. The vrykolkas tradition was so strong on the island of Santorini, where the volcanic soil tended to preserve buried bodies, that the Greeks used the expression "send a vampire to Santorini" as a metaphor for redundant action,

just as the English speak of "carrying coals to Newcastle." Ancient Greeks had buried their dead with an obol in the mouth, a small coin to bar the way to malicious spirits that might try to enter the body. In the nineteenth century, Greeks similarly thwarted vrykolkas by placing a cross of wax or cotton on the lips of the corpse.

Hungarians and Rumanians buried bodies with sickles around their necks, so that if a corpse tried to rise from the grave it would cut off its own head. Rumanians sometimes added the precaution of a sickle through the heart, particularly for the corpses of persons who had never been married and therefore were considered at high risk of becoming *strigoi,* or vampires. Some peoples, including the Finns, restrained corpses by tying their feet or knees together or driving stakes into the grave to pin the body down.

Despite compulsive thirsts, vampires were sometimes thought to be deterred by stratagems that seem almost childlike. Eastern European peasants hung buckthorn and whitethorn—the latter believed to be the shrub from which Jesus' crown was fashioned—on the windows and doors of their houses so that the vampires would become entangled in the thorns and confused. Tradition also had it that millet seeds sprinkled around a grave would force the resident vampire to pick up the seeds rather than search for human victims. Although their breath was said to reek from their foul meals, vampires were thought to dislike strong odors such as that of garlic, so people sometimes put garlic in graves and often wore it about their necks in order to fend off the undead. And like other evil spirits through the ages, vampires were believed to be afraid of silver and representations of the cross, which frequently were hung over doorways or on gates to keep the undead away. People also slept with sharp objects under their pillows to discourage nocturnal visits from vampires or spread human feces on a

cloth and laid it across their chests.

If for some reason corpses were incorrectly buried or the charms failed to ward off vampires, the living were compelled to find the revenants—those who returned from the dead—and destroy them. In some cultures, it was believed that a horse would not step over the grave of a vampire. For this test, the horse had to be all of one color, either black or white, and usually had to be ridden by a virginal youth. In Serbia, the graves of vampires were identified as those falling in upon themselves because they were vacant or those with holes in them from which the vampires escaped. Sometimes vampire hunters had to exhume several bodies and determine which was the vampire by the extent of decay.

Whatever the method of discovery, the means of killing vampires were many and varied, and they included not only driving a stake through the heart but also decapitation, burning, or a combination of all three actions. Some eastern Europeans opened the grave of a suspected vampire, filled it with straw, impaled the body with a stake, then lit the straw and burned the body until it was reduced to a pile of ashes. Often they cut off the corpse's head, usually using a sexton's spade. They then placed the head at the feet of the corpse or behind the buttocks and, for good measure, separated it from the rest of the body by a layer of dirt. Bulgarians and Serbs frequently placed whitethorn in the navel of the corpse and shaved all of the body, with the exception of the head. Then they slit the soles of the feet and drove a nail into the back of the head.

When a stake was driven through a suspected vampire's heart, witnesses frequently averred that the corpse groaned and gushed dark blood. The escape of air remaining in the lungs when a stake was driven into the chest would explain the noise, of course, but it was instead interpreted as a sign that the corpse was still breathing and

In this nineteenth-century painting, a cholera victim lifts the lid from the coffin in which he was prematurely laid.

Such horrifying mistakes were not unknown during epidemics, and they may have contributed to belief in vampirism.

therefore was a vampire. The bloated appearance of the alleged vampires and the signs of blood at the nose and mouth or in the coffin are all considered today to be normal signs of decomposition present about a month after death, the time when most of the bodies were exhumed.

So widespread was the belief in the evil undead predators and so firmly entrenched were the means for warding off and disposing of them that scholars and other writers began to document some of the better-known tales. Charles Ferdinand de Schertz wrote a book called *Magia Posthuma,* which was printed in Czechoslovakia in 1706. De Schertz approached the subject as a lawyer and discussed the facts surrounding reports of vampirism and the legal means of dealing with the creatures. He concluded that the law justified burning their bodies.

In his book, de Schertz tells the tale of a particularly durable vampire who had been a herdsman in the village of Blow near the town Kadam in Bohemia. This herdsman appeared to several people after his death, each of whom died within eight days after his visit. The town inhabitants finally dug up his body and pinned it to the ground with a stake. The herdsman, de Schertz writes, laughed at his would-be exterminators and thanked them for the stick, with which he could defend himself from dogs. The same night, the vampire freed himself from the stake and appeared to several more people, causing further deaths. The townspeople then gave his body to the executioner, who put it in a cart to drive it into town for burning. On the way, the corpse screamed and kicked, flailing about with its arms and legs and generally behaving very much as if alive. When another stake was driven through the herdsman's chest, the body gave a loud cry as fresh blood gushed from the wound. Only after the body was burned to ashes were the villagers able to live in peace.

One of the most famous eighteenth-century accounts of vampirism was that of Arnold Paole, who lived in what is now Yugoslavia. The 1732 document that presented the facts of the case was signed by an Austrian imperial commission of inquiry that consisted of three army surgeons, a

Blaming Vampires for the Black Death

Dead rats dangle from the hat, belt, cuffs, and sword of a peglegged ratcatcher in the seventeenth-century engraving above. Such an eccentric-looking character may have inspired the Pied Piper legend.

"Bring out your dead!" To people living in times of plague, this terrible cry, accompanied by the rumbling of corpse-laden carts, was all too familiar. In the fourteenth century alone, more than a quarter of the population of Europe perished as a result of the disease, which was as mysterious as it was horrifying: Where it might strike and when it might end no one knew. In the face of such uncertainty, superstition thrived and many people blamed the supernatural—vampires especially—for the epidemics.

Early on, a legend arose that the stench of vampires heralded the coming of plague. In 1196, William of Newburgh, an English ecclesiastic and chronicler, blamed an outbreak of the dread disease on a vampire: "The air became foul and tainted as this fetid and corrupting body wandered abroad, so that a terrible plague broke out." The epidemic reputedly ended when two men exhumed the vampire's corpse, drove a spade through it, and burned it. "No sooner had that infernal monster been thus destroyed," William records, "than the plague . . . entirely ceased."

Not until 1898 were the actual culprits exposed. Although people of the Middle Ages had noticed that rats perished in great numbers during times of plague, they assumed that the animals were catching the disease from humans. In fact, people had been contracting plague from virus-carrying fleas that abandoned dead rats in search of new warm-bodied hosts.

Although ignorant of this deadly link, people in earlier centuries abhorred rats all the same. The ubiquitous rodents were called the devil's lap dogs and were said to be familiars of vampires, demons, and witches. The services of ratcatchers were much valued.

An episode in which this relationship was abused is related in the Pied Piper of Hamelin tale. In one version of the story, a ratcatcher—unable to collect his payment—leads the children of Hamelin to Transylvania, the legendary land of vampires.

Some historians also view the tale as an unwitting reference to the role of rats in transmitting the plague. According to this theory, a ratcatcher may have been careless in disposing of the rats he killed in Hamelin. By leaving the carcasses nearby, he may have exposed the children to infection.

Overworked gravediggers find it difficult to keep pace with the rising death toll exacted by the plague in this illustration from a fourteenth-century illuminated manuscript.

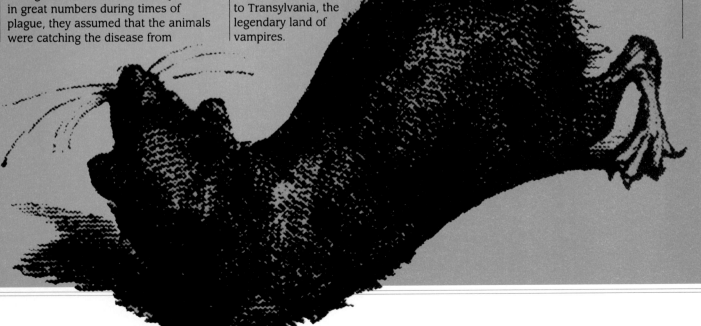

lieutenant colonel, and a sublieutenant. In Paole's time, his region was under Hapsburg rule. The Catholic Hapsburgs considered the Orthodox Serbs and Hungarians of the area to be schismatics and collaborators with the empire's Turkish enemy, and one way for the Catholic church to impress its spiritual influence on the people was to hunt down and destroy the vampires in which they believed. In fact, many of those accused of being vampires were—like Peter Plogojowitz—Slavs of Orthodox persuasion.

Paole was a young man who returned to his native village of Meduegna, near Belgrade, after military service in the Levant in the spring of 1727. He settled down, bought a cottage and two acres of land, fell in love, and betrothed himself to a young woman named Nina, daughter of a rich neighboring farmer.

Although Paole was always cordial in his dealings with the locals, they felt there was something strange about him. Nina also sensed that Paole was troubled, and she asked him what was oppressing him. Paole told her that he was haunted by the fear of a premature death, an apprehension that had begun to trouble him after he had a strange adventure during his army service in Greece. He had been visited by an undead being, Paole told his fiancée, but he had found its unhallowed grave and dealt with the body in hopes that he could ward off its evil. That was why he had resigned from the military and returned to his village at such a young age.

For a time it seemed as though Paole had escaped the effects of the vampire. Then, during harvest time, he fell from a hay wagon, was injured, and died. About a month

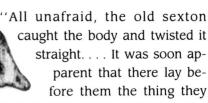

later, rumors began to circulate in the village that Paole had been seen wandering around after nightfall. People complained that he haunted them, and several died. It seemed that after all, Arnold Paole had not been able to escape the curse of the vampire. After about two and a half months, villagers decided they should disinter Paole's body.

In this engraving, Transylvanian coffin makers finish a casket with silver nails. This practice drew on the belief that vampires feared the precious metal.

The party that gathered around his grave was led by two military officers sent out from Belgrade, where reports of the events had stirred official interest. The officers were joined by two Army surgeons, a drummer boy who carried their instrument cases, and an old sexton and his assistants. When they opened the casket of Arnold Paole, they found that "the corpse had moved to one side, the jaws gaped wide open and the blue lips were moist with new blood which had trickled in a thin stream from the corner of the mouth," according to the report of the imperial inquiry.

"All unafraid, the old sexton caught the body and twisted it straight. . . . It was soon apparent that there lay before them the thing they dreaded—the vampire. He looked, indeed, as if he had not been dead a day." As the sexton handled the corpse its outer skin came off and below there were new skin and new nails.

Fear seized the men. The drummer boy swooned at the first sight of the vampire. The others scattered garlic over the body and drove a stake through it, upon which the corpse gave a terrible shriek and gushed blood in "a great crimson jet." They also exhumed the bodies of the four people believed to have been killed by Paole and drove whitethorn stakes through them, to prevent their returning as vampires. Then they burned all five corpses and buried the ashes in consecrated ground.

For a time it seemed that these measures had worked. Reports of vampirism in the village subsided. But five years

Buried in England more than 400 years ago, a skeleton lies riveted to its coffin at the joints of the body. The deceased may have been suspected of being a witch and thus considered a likely candidate for a restless death.

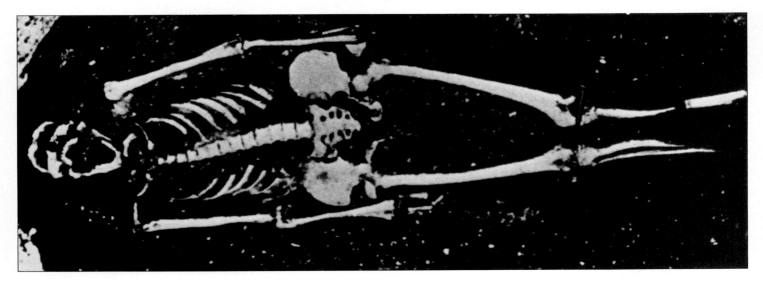

after the first rash of deaths, several people died, it was said, from a mysterious loss of blood, and rumors of vampires again swept through the neighborhood. The authorities appointed a commission of inquiry, whose investigations included opening the graves of recently deceased people and performing a medical examination of the exhumed bodies. The commission's reports, dated 1732, cited some extraordinary findings: plump, healthy-looking bodies of women and children who had died months earlier, although the corpses of others who had expired at the same time were already in a state of advanced decomposition. The commission's agents transfixed all the suspicious corpses with stakes, then decapitated and burned them. Apparently that quelled the outbreak.

Much of the surviving information on vampires of this period was compiled by Dom Augustin Calmet, a French Benedictine monk and biblical scholar. For several years, this studious and religious man collected reports of alleged cases of vampirism, and in 1746, he published a book whose French title translates as "Dissertation upon the Apparitions of Angels, Demons and Ghosts, and of Revenants and Vampires of Hungary, Bohemia, Moravia and Silesia." An English version of the work, published thirteen years later, earned a wide audience because it was written from a Christian point of view.

Calmet, who said he wanted to apply reason to the question and determine for the Church's sake whether vampires were real, approached the subject with trepidation. "Those who believe them to be true, will accuse me of rashness and presumption, for having raised a doubt on the subject, or even of having denied their existence and reality; others will blame me for having employed my time in discussing this matter which is considered as frivolous and useless by many sensible people," he wrote. "Whatever may be thought of it, I shall be pleased with myself for having sounded a question which appeared to me important in a religious point of view."

Dom Calmet set out to explain some of the more puzzling aspects of vampirism: How, he wondered, was it possible for a corpse to leave its grave through four or five feet of earth? Or was it the ghost of the corpse that appeared to the living, leaving the body behind? What gave the corpses their evil energy? Why were the exhumed bodies of suspected vampires "ruddy and lifelike?"

Calmet told the story of a soldier, quartered in a peasant household on the frontiers of Hungary, who sat down for a meal with his landlord's family. A man the soldier had not met came in and sat down with them, which, strangely, terrified everyone present, especially the landlord. The soldier did not know what to make of the situation. The next day, his landlord died and when the soldier asked what had happened, he was told that the peasant's father, who had been dead and buried for more than ten years, was the man who had come in and sat down at the table, bringing the son news of his own impending death. The father, obviously, had become a vampire.

When the soldier told the story to his superiors, a captain in the regiment, the count de Cabreras, was assigned to investigate the incident. Accompanied by several other officers, a surgeon, and a notary, the count visited the peasants' house and was told by the entire family that the man who had sat with them at the table was indeed the landlord's father—long dead, but now undead. The villagers dug up the body of the father, and it was found to be "in the same state as if it has been but just dead, the blood like that of a living person." The count ordered the head to be cut off, and the corpse was reburied. The investigation progressed to depositions about other vampires, including a man who had been dead and buried for more than thirty years. In all, three suspected vampires were dug up and dealt with by decapitation, driving a nail through the temple, or burning.

After pulling together his exhaustive compilation of vampire reports—some of them, such as the notarized statements collected by the count de Cabreras, well documented—Calmet concluded: "The particulars which are related are so singular . . . accompanied with . . . most weighty and well-attested legal depositions that it seems impossible not to subscribe to the belief." However, he maintained a degree of skepticism, arguing that hasty burial of people in comas, trances, or the paralyzing grip of severe illness probably accounted for some cases. And he called the practice of mutilating and burning the bodies of such victims "a great wrong" and was puzzled that the authorities allowed it to continue.

More than a century after Dom Augustin Calmet focused his attentions on how "flesh-and-blood" vampires could overcome the restrictions of the grave, a Frenchman named Adolphe d'Assier, a member of the Bordeaux Academy of Sciences, came to the conclusion that the bodies of vampires were sustained by a "fluidic being," an entity that "assumes charge of the functions" that the living individual performed previously. In his 1887 treatise on phantoms, *Posthumous Humanity,* d'Assier explained that the vampire specter became a "nocturnal marauder . . . on behalf of its old landlord."

"Thenceforth the struggle for existence continues beyond the tomb with the same tenacity, the same brutal and selfish ferocity, one might say the same cynicism, as in living nature," he wrote. He deduced that the blood sucked by the spirit immediately passed into the body's organs, preventing decay and preserving the suppleness of the limbs and ruddiness of the flesh. Only by disinterring and burning the body could the deadly cycle be broken, he wrote.

Somewhat later, a famous and eccentric English scholar, Montague Summers, devoted a great portion of his life to the study of "the monstrous things that lie only just beneath the surface of our cracking civilization," including vampirism. Although the century he worked in—the twentieth—was probably less receptive to the notion of vampires than were the eras of his predecessors in the field, Summers became perhaps the best-known

A Royal Attack on Fear and Superstition

Amid the dark ignorance of eighteenth-century central Europe, one woman was a beacon of reason. She was Maria Theresa, archduchess of Austria, queen of Hungary and Bohemia. In January 1755, she learned of a vampire scare in the province of Moravia: With approval of the clergy, people there were exhuming the bodies of alleged vampires, and on finding some corpses well-preserved, hacking and burning them.

The queen dispatched her physician, a respected scientist named Gerard van Swieten, to investigate. Van Swieten's report detailed nonmysterious explanations for corpses failing to decompose, including dry earth and tightly closed coffins. One case was that of

Rosina Polackin, a woman who had been pronounced a vampire by local medics after they had examined her unputrified corpse. "What ignorance!" sighed van Swieten, noting that Polackin's body was buried in December and dug up in January and had remained frozen the whole time.

His report prompted the queen to issue a landmark document in the struggle against superstition, her 1755 edict on vampires. It forbade traditional procedures and decreed that allegations about revenants were to be reported to civil authorities, not the Church. But even her decree could not defeat age-old fears; vampire hunts continued, albeit more discreetly. As recently as 1912, Hungarian farmers dealt with the corpse of a suspected vampire in the time-honored—and outlawed—fashion.

student of vampirism of all time. In his studies, *The Vampire, His Kith and Kin* and *The Vampire in Europe,* Summers applied scholarly techniques and extensive documentation to tales of vampirism.

Taken in their totality, Summers's efforts form a kind of core of modern research into transformation of all kinds. His interest and belief not only in vampirism but in lycanthropy and witchcraft as well were so intense that they were said to be paradoxically the reason that he abandoned the Church of England, in which he was an ordained deacon, to become a Roman Catholic: He needed what he considered to be the stronger "magic" of Catholic ritual to combat such evil powers. An authority on the literature of the English Restoration period, Summers was highly respected by fellow scholars despite his penchant for dressing up in the long frock coats, purple stockings, and buckled shoes of that seventeenth-century era, his hair styled and curled to give the appearance of a short wig. Never one to avoid being noticed, he was often seen carrying an ebony cane with a silver handle that upon closer inspection turned out to be "an extremely immodest representation" of Zeus in the form of a swan ravishing the beauteous Leda.

Summers was born into a well-off and evangelically pious family in Clifton, an elegant suburb outside Bristol in southwestern England, on April 10, 1880. He developed an early taste for the literature of the sixteenth and seventeenth centuries in the well-stocked library of Tellisford House, the imposing family home. He studied at Clifton College, where he read widely in obscure subjects and became interested in Catholicism, in spite of the family's Protestant background. In 1899, he entered Trinity College, Oxford, where he burned incense in his rooms and became known as a "character." He went on to study at Lichfield Theological College and was ordained as an Anglican deacon in 1908. Summers was appointed to a curacy in the Bristol suburb of Bitton, but he left there under a dark cloud when, with another clergyman, he was accused of pederasty, a charge of which he was subsequently acquitted.

After he left Bitton, Summers turned to the darker subjects that had long fascinated him, including vampirism, and converted to the Roman church in 1909. He may also have received holy orders. At least he called himself the Reverend Alphonsus Joseph-Mary Augustus Montague Summers and maintained in his home a private oratory, or prayer chapel. Reviewers of his *History of Witchcraft and Demonology,* said one writer, "were astounded to find that its author appeared to believe utterly in the Devil as the prime mover of all evil, including witchcraft, and to share every last medieval superstition he described." He went on to edit and translate earlier works on witchcraft, two of which were confiscated by the police on the charge of obscenity. Both books were ordered destroyed after an inquiry in 1934. Although the tone of Summers's works was always one of passionate indignation, a story began to spread that he had participated in a Black Mass in 1913. Summers spent considerable time in France and Italy "for health reasons," he said, which added to speculation that he dabbled in the occult on the Continent.

Before his death in 1948, Summers lived quietly in various cities in England, writing his own books and amassing a vast library of other volumes touching upon bizarre and sinister subjects. At Oxford, where he lived for a time and did research at the Bodleian Library, he was regarded by many people as "a kind of clerical Doctor Faustus," according to a contemporary. It was whispered in Oxford that one often could see Summers walking with his secretary, Summers walking with his dog, or the secretary walking with the dog, but that one never saw the three together—implying, perhaps in jest, a classic case of multiple shapeshifting. Whatever the truth about Montague Summers, his life was a puzzling mixture of ardent faith in the teachings of the Catholic church and an equally strong, perhaps unholy, fascination with evil.

Montague Summers found from his extensive researches that not all stories of vampires—not even the grimmest ones—involved revenants, beings who returned from the grave. The darker annals of civilization, as well as the newspapers of his own era, were dotted with accounts of actual, living people who were termed vampires because of their seemingly insatiable desire for human blood or flesh. This particular category of vampire, Summers noted, includes such diverse examples as a fourteen-year-old French girl known for greedily sucking recently inflicted wounds, an Italian bandit by the name of Gaetano Mammone, who "was accustomed as a regular habit to drain with his lips the blood of his unhappy captives," and innumerable cannibals down through the ages. It also includes those who defile the dead rather than attack the living to satisfy their unnatural cravings. "Vampirism," said Summers, "in its extended and more modern sense, may be understood to mean any profanation of a dead body"—compared with which, he suggested, "there can be nothing more horrible, no crime more repellent."

The truth of that last contention seems particularly vulnerable to challenge when one considers how repellent have been the crimes of some living vampires who murdered their victims rather than merely disinterring their bodies. One of the most notorious of all time was a sixteenth-century Hungarian noblewoman, the countess Elizabeth Báthory, who became widely known as the Blood Countess. Her story reads like the wilder imaginings of a horror-movie scriptwriter but in fact is taken from transcripts of official interrogations and testimony at a trial that took place after authorities finally caught up with her. The trial documents became part of the Budapest State Archives.

Elizabeth Báthory was born in 1560 in a great castle in northwestern Hungary, in the shadows of the Carpathian Mountain foothills near Transylvania. Her family was one of the country's most prominent and powerful, but through the generations ran a wide streak of madness and a taste for decadence; the family tree was festooned with well-known sexual deviates, sadists and masochists, Satanists, poisoners, heretics, and intellectuals.

At age eleven, Elizabeth was betrothed to Ferencz Nádasdy, the scion of another prominent Protestant family. Her father had recently died, and her mother sent her to live with the Nádasdy family, where she would be trained for her future role as a countess. By all accounts a precocious child, Elizabeth soon became bored with the domestic routine and found secret thrills in playing with the peasant boys on the estate; by age thirteen she was pregnant by one of them. Her mother retrieved her under the guise of an illness, and she went into seclusion at one of the more remote Báthory castles. The newborn child was spirited out of the country, and shortly after Elizabeth's fifteenth birthday, she married Ferencz Nádasdy.

Although the newlyweds had the choice of several more salubrious houses in which to make their new home, the countess chose the dank and gloomy Csejthe Castle, in a setting bordered by thick forests where wolves howled at night. Her new husband was soon off campaigning in lengthy wars, and she was left to her own devices at the castle. She whiled away her time engaging in affairs with various men and soon discovered that she found pleasure in inflicting pain on servant girls, especially if they were bosomy and younger than eighteen. Her husband, himself known for his delight in torturing Turkish captives, expressed no objection to his wife's cruelties to the lowly peasant girls, and the couple lived happily enough, producing four children between 1585 and 1595.

When Ferencz died during the winter of 1604, his widow was freed of marital concerns and could concentrate on new and inventive ways to pleasure herself through others' pain. She elaborated on the frequent beatings that she and some trusted members of her household staff administered to her victims, adding various kinds of humiliations and tortures, including pressing red-hot coins and keys into the hands of the hapless girls. The countess, a vain and beautiful woman always searching for new potions that would preserve her youth, engaged a magician named Anna Darvulia to concoct magic elixirs for her. One day a servant girl bled profusely when struck by Báthory, and the blood splashed onto the countess. Báthory noticed to her im-

In a photo from the 1930s, "vampirologist" Montague Summers poses in the biretta and black robe of a Roman Catholic priest. Catholicism appealed to the former Anglican deacon, who believed that its rituals were very effective against the powers of evil. To Summers, vampires and werewolves were "monstrous things that lie only just beneath the surface of our cracking civilization."

mense delight that when she wiped off the blood, her skin seemed softer and whiter. She believed she had discovered the secret to remaining young: She must bathe frequently in human blood.

Before long the countess and her helpers—a nanny, a wet nurse, and a valet—began carrying their torture sessions to fatal extremes in the dungeons of her several homes. Their activities were so vilely obscene as to beggar description. A single example will suffice. The countess installed in the cellar of her Vienna mansion a cylindrical iron cage with metal spikes pointing inward, a kind of loose-fitting iron maiden. After a girl or young woman was locked into it, the cage was hoisted to the ceiling. One of the torturers then prodded the victim with a red-hot poker, causing her to flail about against the spikes, while the countess sat below showering in—and, it was said, drinking—the blood. After a time, when the countess's blood baths failed to stem the onslaught of middle age, she turned to blue-blooded victims, young ladies of noble birth, a supply much more difficult to maintain.

Disposing of bodies without attracting anyone's attention always presented a problem, but it grew to be virtually impossible during the height of the countess's madness with the spiked cage in Vienna, when her helpers were forced to simply dump the drained victims in a field. Terrified villagers in the vicinity believed that a plague of vampirism was responsible for the bloodless corpses that kept turning up—and in the broad sense of the word they were, of course, correct.

Eventually, rumors of the horrifying rituals became persistent and widespread. After the bodies of four victims were dumped below the Csejthe Castle ramparts, frightened villagers who had long suspected Báthory were emboldened to complain to authorities. Around Christmas of 1610, Báthory was formally questioned by her cousin, the lord palatine of Hungary, Count György Thurzo, who was anxious to preserve the family from disgrace. The Blood Countess's accomplices were arrested and confessed to the murders. A witness for the prosecution testified that he had seen a list

A Theory about the Thirst for Blood

Mystical healing properties have long been attributed to human blood *(below, magnified 250 times).* In bygone times, people imbibed the fluid in desperate attempts to cure their afflictions. One modern researcher, however, has speculated that in some cases the desire to consume blood may have been a symptom of a disease and that the so-called vampires of history may have suffered from it. The condition, porphyria, is a rare, inherited blood disorder characterized by anemia. Porphyria is now treatable, but the researcher theorizes that the urge to overcome the effects of severe anemia may have driven some earlier sufferers to drink blood. Symptoms of the disease include extreme sensitivity to sunlight and a retraction of the gums that exposes the teeth—classic vampire traits.

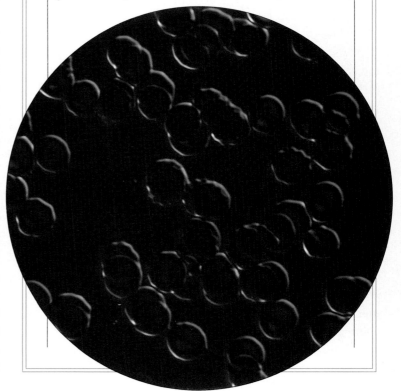

written by the countess of the girls and young women who had been killed, putting their number at no fewer than 650.

After a five-day trial, in which Báthory's name was mentioned only once, her helpers were sentenced to be publicly tortured and put to death. The countess herself was never tried, but was quietly locked away in her own bedroom in Csejthe Castle. Workmen walled up the room's windows and doors, and there the prisoner was confined, with only a food hatch connecting her to the outside world. She died there on August 21, 1614. The only words about Báthory that had slipped into the trial proceedings called her "a bloodthirsty, and blood-sucking Godless woman caught in the act at Csejthe Castle."

As awful as were the deeds of the bloody countess, in the centuries since then other "living vampires" have committed acts that seemed no less sensational and frightening to the people, even if in retrospect they pale beside Báthory's excesses in unrelieved evil. One case that terrified France in the middle of the nineteenth century involved a mysterious night creature who ripped corpses from their graves. The elusiveness of this nocturnal prowler, who seemed not to be deterred by high walls or guards, caused the public to believe a supernatural being was responsible— "the vampire of Paris," as the malefactor was dubbed by the newspapers of the day.

The "vampire" first surfaced in 1849, when guards at Paris's Père Lachaise Cemetery, the final resting place of many famous painters, musicians, and writers, began to catch glimpses of a shadowy figure flitting among the tombstones at night. On a number of mornings they discovered graves and tombs desecrated, the bodies dumped from their coffins and savagely attacked. The authorities, who themselves apparently fueled the newspaper headlines by applying the term vampirism to the case, were unable to catch the culprit. After more graves were disturbed at Montparnasse Cemetery in Paris and at a suburban burial ground, people began to speculate that a phantom vampire was responsible. After all, the high walls of the cemeteries had heavy iron gates that were kept locked after nightfall.

Faced with increasing public fear, authorities called in the military, and one night not much later, soldiers lying in ambush at Montparnasse Cemetery thought that they spied something in the distance, moving among the graves. Soon they heard the sound of wood being ripped apart. At that, the commander of the group barked an order that sent the men rushing through the tombstones toward the source of the noise. In the darkness, a figure broke cover and darted for the perimeter of the cemetery. Gunshots rang out, but the fleeing figure managed to scramble over the high wall and disappear. When the soldiers inspected the fugitive's trail by lantern light, however, they discovered traces of blood and a scrap of military uniform.

Knowing now that they were seeking a soldier with an unexplained fresh wound, authorities easily tracked down Sergeant Victor Bertrand. Bertrand, a handsome, well-groomed, blond young man, confessed to an "irresistible impulse" to prowl cemeteries. But he said he was hardly conscious of what acts he was committing once he got there. The trial of Victor Bertrand on July 10, 1849, drew a glittering audience of Parisian high society. He was judged to be sane but, because he had not physically harmed any living person, was sentenced to only a year's imprisonment.

During his term in prison, Bertrand wrote a full account of what he had done. After his release, the public never heard from him again.

If the term vampire seems loosely applied in Bertrand's case, it appears somewhat more appropriate to describe a German named Fritz Haarmann, who in the 1920s became notorious as the Hannover Vampire. Haarmann was the youngest child of a rough, foul-tempered locomotive fireman and, according to "vampirologist" Montague Summers, grew up in the industrial city of Hannover hating and fearing his father. As a youth he was accused of molesting children, but because he was "dull and stupid," the court decided he was not responsible for his deeds and sent him to an insane asylum.

Haarmann escaped and eventually returned home, where he remained until frequent violent quarrels with his father drove him to enlist in the army. Discharged from the service on account of illness, he returned again to Hannover and was arrested there several times—for fraud and burglary, as well as for indecent exposure. After a spell in prison, he was released in 1918 and seemed to start a new, respectable life for himself. He opened a small shop that sold sausages and cooked meats, enjoying excellent business in the time of scarcity that followed Germany's defeat in World War I. And he became a police buff and informant, helping Hannover detectives with tips about the city's petty criminals. He apparently took pleasure in hearing the hausfraus lined up at his shop refer to him in whispers as Detective Haarmann.

He also used his entrée with the police to facilitate the monstrous acts he was later found to have committed. Hannover's main railway station was continually crowded with homeless boys and young men moving from city to city in a largely futile search for work. Because the policemen on du-

Radiating sadistic pleasure, Elizabeth Báthory looks on as her servants drag naked peasant girls into the snow and douse them with water. According to testimony that inspired this nineteenth-century painting, the victims literally froze to death.

Nature's Own Nocturnal Blood Drinkers

Although the existence of vampires who rise from the grave has never been proved, there does exist a creature who feeds exclusively on blood. The vampire bat has several traits in common with the revenants of lore, whose name it was given when it was discovered in the New World. The bat too passes days in darkness, venturing from its hideaway—usually a cave or mine—only under cover of night. And, like the bloodsuckers of the movies, the bat may return to the same victim night after night. But although humans sometimes get bitten, sleeping cows and chickens are more typical sources of nourishment for vampire bats.

Native to South and Central America, the tiny mammals daily consume their weight in blood—an ounce to an ounce and a half. They alight or crawl on dozing victims, slice through the flesh with sharp incisors, then lick up—not suck—the trickle of blood. Vampire bats can kill their prey, but not by draining the blood. The danger posed by the bats is that they will infect their food sources with diseases such as rabies.

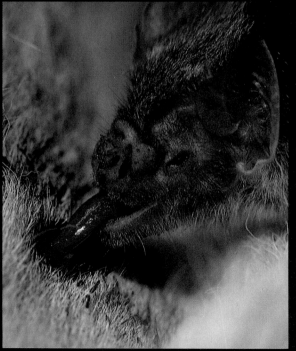

After scraping a sleeping calf's skin with its sharp teeth, a vampire bat laps blood from the wound. An anticoagulant in its saliva ensures a free-flowing feast.

ty there knew Haarmann as an ally, he was free to prowl the third-class waiting room in the middle of the night. He would awaken some youth among the scores that were sleeping on the floor, demand in an official manner to see a ticket, ask sharp questions about the boy's place of origin and his destination, then in a sudden turn to sympathetic generosity, dangle promises of a bed and a hot meal that often convinced the weary lad to leave the station and go home with him.

Even those sufficiently experienced and cynical to believe they knew what price Haarmann would extract from them in exchange for his hospitality really had no idea, or they would never have accompanied him. For in the privacy of his rooms behind the shop, Haarmann—a heavy man and apparently a strong one—would contrive to pin down his victim and then suddenly sink his teeth into the youth's exposed throat in a fatal bite. Few nightmares could produce a vampire more vicious than this living one.

In what must have been an intensely suspenseful encounter for the murderer, Haarmann's career as a vampire came within a hair's breadth—or more exactly, the thickness of a newspaper—of being stopped by police almost as soon as it began. As far as could be determined later, his first victim was a seventeen-year-old runaway named Friedel Rothe. Friedel had mailed a postcard to his mother, who received it at about the time her beloved son was falling prey to Haarmann. Knowing from the postmark that Friedel was in Hannover, the Rothes tracked down his acquaintances there, who told them their son had accepted an offer of a place to stay from a ''detective.''

Under pressure from the Rothes, Hannover police deduced that the so-called detective might have been Haarmann and went to his residence. When they burst in unannounced, they surprised Haarmann in an act of ''gross indecency'' with another boy and had no choice but to arrest him. They did not thoroughly search the premises, however, so they did not find the severed head of Friedel Rothe, which—as Haarmann revealed years later—''was hidden under a newspaper behind the oven. Later on, I threw it into the canal." Instead of being revealed as a killer, Haarmann served nine months for gross indecency and resumed his horrifying practices.

By official count, his deadly teeth claimed at least twenty-four victims before he was caught, although some people who studied the case thought the number might be nearer to fifty. The oldest killed was eighteen years of age, the youngest just twelve. Haarmann collaborated with an accomplice named Hans Grans during much of his seven-year murder spree. Grans, a handsome young man who seemed totally devoid of conscience, frequently brought in the candidates for Haarmann's fatal attentions. He induced Haarmann to commit one murder because he, Grans, wanted the youth's new trousers, another because he coveted the victim's fancy shirt.

Haarmann's practice of disposing of body parts in the waterway behind his home ultimately helped lead to his undoing; a number of skulls and bones found there in the spring of 1924 turned the spotlight of suspicion toward him. Shortly thereafter, it focused sharply on him when he tried to pick up a young man by the name of Fromm at the railway station. Fromm objected noisily and shouted accusations of indecency. Police, who arrested both men, searched Haarmann's place and discovered several bodies in varied states of dismemberment. Haarmann admitted to twenty-seven murders; however, the police apparently could not assemble corroborating evidence for some of them. Yet the actual number of homicides probably did not stun and sicken the citizens of Hannover as much as did one detail of his confession: Fritz Haarmann had ground parts of some of the victims into sausages, which he not only ate himself but also sold to his customers.

At his trial in 1924 on twenty-four counts of murder, Haarmann insisted he was sane but claimed he was always in a trance when he committed the killings. The judge rejected this argument out of hand, citing the concentrated effort needed to hold the victims down while biting their throats. He sentenced Haarmann to death, and the accomplice Grans to life imprisonment. Although the court took no official cognizance of the talk of vampirism that had swept Hannover following the revelations, the death sentence ordered was decapitation.

On April 15, 1925, the neck of the Vampire of Hannover was sundered by the razor-sharp blade of a heavy sword, a most unusual means of execution for twentieth-century Europe, but one that Montague Summers, at least, found not too surprising. "It was perhaps something more than mere coincidence that the mode of execution should be the severing of the head from the body," he pointed out, "since this was one of the efficacious methods of destroying a vampire."

As the twentieth century has lurched along its tumultuous course, cases of mass murders on a scale similar to that of Fritz Haarmann's crimes have become, if not commonplace, at least distressingly familiar in the Western world. In the 1940s, an Englishman named John George Haigh was put to death for murder after confessing to killing nine people, drinking their blood, then dissolving their bodies in acid; inevitably, Fleet Street dubbed him the Acid Bath Vampire. In the late 1950s, a quiet bachelor recluse, Eddie Gein, was found to have skins, heads, and other parts of at least ten corpses in his tumble-down Wisconsin farmhouse. He admitted to murdering two people, claiming he acquired the other grisly mementos by graverobbing. Throughout the 1960s, 1970s, and 1980s, serial killers and mass murderers have crowded the news—the Charles Manson Family, the Yorkshire Ripper, the Boston Strangler and Los Angeles's Hillside Strangler, the Green River Killer, John Gacy, Charles Starkweather, Ted Bundy, and other names that come to the attention of a shocked public, then fade before an onrush of new candidates for grim notoriety.

Of course, none of these murderers are nowadays spo-

Delving through debris at the vacant Sussex factory where John George Haigh murdered nine victims and disposed of their bodies, British police search for evidence to convict the so-called Acid Bath Vampire. Although many people believed that the debt-ridden Haigh (inset, center figure) was motivated purely by greed, he denied the characterization: "It was not their money but their blood that I was after."

ken of as vampires—not in any serious sense, anyway; headline writers may reach for the term for its sensational value, as they did in the case of the Acid Bath Vampire, but they do not expect it to be taken literally. Now such killers are described instead as disturbed, mentally ill, sociopathic, or just downright evil. People tend to regard them as a strictly modern phenomenon, by-products of our unnatural, stress-skewed society.

And yet their behavior is not really new. It is similar to that which we used to ascribe—mistakenly—to wild animals: killing viciously and wantonly, not for survival but for thrills, or to satisfy some dark and unexplained inner need.

In many respects, this seems to be the very behavior that in centuries past characterized people who consequently were believed to be real vampires or werewolves. Is it possible that perhaps the world has not changed so much as we think? That the killer who stalks helpless children with a semiautomatic assault rifle today is basically the same breed as the person whose slaughter of innocents in seventeenth-century Europe would cause neighbors to believe he had been supernaturally transformed into a werewolf or a vampire?

Meanwhile, the vampire that glides from the pages of books or from the movie screen to grip the popular imagination today has become a very different creature altogether, more likely to be a sleekly handsome, fascinating, and perhaps even sympathetic aristocrat than a deceased peasant who crawls from the grave a bloodthirsty monster, probably more involved with a mysterious mix of the allures of sex and romantic death than with gruesome murder and the stench of rotting flesh.

This more attractive vampire is of relatively recent origins, having come to life in the so-called Gothic literature of the eighteenth and nineteenth centuries, a movement heavy with macabre themes, mysterious settings, and the supernatural. He can be said to have been born in 1819 with the publication of *The Vampyre* by Dr. John Polidori.

Polidori, a Scot of Italian extraction, was the personal physician of one of the most influential literary figures of his day, the romantic poet George Gordon, Lord Byron. In the summer of 1816, Polidori vacationed near

In an illustration taken from Varney the Vampire, the accursed protagonist seizes his swooning victim, holds her down, and prepares to plunge his teeth into her throat. Such titillating episodes enhanced the appeal of that nineteenth-century penny serial.

Geneva, Switzerland, in the illustrious company of Byron, poet Percy Bysshe Shelley, and Shelley's wife, Mary Wollstonecraft Shelley. To relieve the boredom of a rainy week in June, Byron proposed that each member of the party write a horror story. From this suggestion grew Mary Shelley's *Frankenstein.* Byron sketched plans for a vampire tale but never finished it. Instead, Polidori wrote the story. At the time the story was published, rumors circulated that it was the work of Byron, and it was widely read throughout Europe.

Polidori's protagonist was named Lord Ruthven, a libertine who was modeled loosely on Lord Byron. Although Lord Ruthven dresses, speaks, and acts like those around him, there is something mysterious and dangerously threatening about him. Like the literary vampires that followed him, he is repulsive and attractive at the same time. Lord Ruthven provides society with a welcome diversion during a bleak London winter. "His peculiarities caused him to be invited to every house; all wished to see him, and those who had been accustomed to violent excitement, and now felt the weight of ennui, were pleased at having something in their presence capable of engaging their attention," John Polidori wrote. "In spite of the deadly hue of his face, which never gained a warmer tint, either from the blush of modesty, or from the strong emotion of passion, though its form and outline were beautiful, many of the female hunters after notoriety attempted to win his attention."

Thirty years after *The Vampyre,* the publishing house of Edward Lloyd brought out 220 lurid chapters of *Varney the Vampire,* subtitled *The Feast of Blood.* This was a so-called penny-dreadful novel, targeted at a mass audience and published in 1847 in installments decorated with covers that combined horror with lurid sex. Like many Gothic "bloods," the story is thought to have been written by several collaborating authors. The

868-page tale firmly planted the staples of vampire lore in the minds of its enthusiastic readers: the vampire's middle-European background, the initiation of the heroine through sex, and imaginative if scientifically unfounded "medical" explanations for vampirism. Despite his evil doings, Varney the vampire is portrayed as a basically good person driven to evil by forces beyond his control. He tries to save himself but despairs and commits suicide by jumping into the crater of Mount Vesuvius.

The most important vampire of literature, of course, the figure whose vast shadow defines the entire genre, is Count Dracula of Transylvania, the creation of Irish author Bram Stoker. First published in 1897, the novel *Dracula* was instantly popular and has never been out of print. In this book, Stoker focused the vampire legend and set it firmly in Transylvania, where Count Dracula lived in a ruined castle.

Stoker also quite literally gave shape to the very shadow that Dracula casts—the author was apparently the first to create a vampire character that was able to transform himself into a bat.

Although Stoker made his living as a clerk in Ireland and later as a London theater director, he wrote continuously and published many Gothic novels and short stories before the idea for Dracula took shape in his mind. The seed was planted in 1890, when he met a University of Budapest professor of oriental languages, Arminius Vämbery, who had come to Stoker's theater for a performance and later joined the writer-director for dinner.

Vämbery talked at length about the history and literature of central Europe and told engrossing tales of a fifteenth-century warrior and tyrant by the name of Dracula, also known as Vlad the Impaler *(pages 104-107).* The stories impressed Stoker, who later wrote to Vämbery to request more information on Dracula. He also delved into the British Museum, ferreting out details about Transylvania and the despot who was notorious for his cruel rule. Stoker's research was to make the novel's background material amazingly accurate for fiction of that era. But to create the title character, he exercised extensive artistic license, for there had never been any suggestion that the real-life Dracula was a vampire.

Stoker's fictional Dracula is an aristocrat who wants to purchase some property in England for mysterious reasons. The vampire-count engages the services of a young British real estate agent by the name of Jonathan Harker, then imprisons him because the Englishman has seen too many secrets in Dracula's Transylvanian castle. Dracula then emigrates to England, feasting on the ship's crew during the voyage. Once in Britain, the seductive count manages to sink his fangs into the tender throats of several swooning women, one of them Harker's fiancée. In accordance with eastern European tradition, the bites taint all of the victims with vampire blood.

But he is pursued by a professor who knows about vampires, including the vital information that a vampire cannot survive in sunlight and therefore only stirs from his coffin at night. This hero and Harker, who has escaped from the castle, eventually catch up with Dracula as the sun is setting and manage to slash his throat and plunge a knife into his heart before he can rise from his coffin to harm them. Before their eyes, the terrible fiend dissolves into dust, upon his face "a look of peace, such as I never could have imagined might have rested there."

Part of the appeal of *Dracula,* especially in the superficially repressed Victorian world in which it was first published, was the book's overtly sensual overtones. The evil count had a mesmerizing effect on those models of virtue who fell under his spell—especially women. He paralyzed them with his intense stare, seducing them into joining him in his undead state.

The strong sexual element evident in the book was not new. Throughout the ages, the fear and revulsion that the notion of vampires inspires have been mixed with a strangely tenacious physical attraction. Perhaps because vampires were generally believed to strike while their victims were sleeping, vulnerable and in their beds, vampire attacks always have been closely associated with sexual activity. The human acts of kissing, sucking, and biting are closely related from infancy and together have a sexual significance that in tales of vampirism is perverted into a death kiss. Traditionally, newly created vampires turned on their spouses or lovers as their first victims. Consequently, the widows or widowers of suspected vampires were the first to be questioned by authorities when an epidemic of vampirism broke out.

Many of the vampires and vampirelike creatures of folklore were thought capable of impregnating women. Belief in the dreaded incubus and succubus—male and female spirits who visited people in the night and engaged in vigorous, debilitating sex—was closely related to belief in vampirism. The bloodthirsty lamias of Greek legend sexually seduced their victims before sucking their blood. The nosferat of Rumanian superstition was an illegitimate stillborn child

Psychic Variations on an Old Theme

Although the word *vampire* usually conjures up visions of sanguivorous corpses returned to cause havoc among the living, in the last hundred years or so the term has assumed more subtle meanings as well. At some point in the past, students of the supernatural began cautioning against another kind of vampire—one who did not exactly thirst for blood but was nevertheless to be feared.

"Even without any actual sucking of blood," wrote twentieth-century vampirologist Montague Summers, "there is a vampire who can—consciously, or perhaps unconsciously—support his life and re-energize his frame by drawing upon the vitality of others." Summers labeled this singularly parasitic personality type as a "spiritual vampire" and a "psychic sponge." He described

an individual who inevitably left companions feeling weary and spiritless, as if all available vital energy had been soaked away.

Some students of the occult go so far as to warn that psychic vampires are everywhere in society and that even though they may not inflict direct physical harm, they are nonetheless potentially dangerous. To protect against spiritual leeching, one believer recommends clenching the hands while walking down the street, so that the life force cannot leak through the fingers to be lapped up by passing psychic vampires. Another proposed defense is to imagine oneself surrounded by a dense, white mist, which will purportedly serve as a shield against the energy pirates.

A variation on the psychic vampire is

the so-called vamp. More a product of Hollywood than of the occult, the term was coined by publicists to promote the 1914 silent-film debut of actress Theda Bara *(below)*, the original silver-screen femme fatale. Although her kohl-darkened eyes and deathly pale skin fit the physical description of the classic fiend, Bara typically played the role of a figurative vampire. The actress often portrayed the seductive adventuress who latched on to vulnerable men, bleeding them dry of money and possessions, and leaving them pitiful shells of their former selves. Audiences flocked to theaters to leer or hiss at the cruel, sexy, exotic-looking Bara. In more than thirty films, she thrived not on her victims' blood but on the sheer perverse pleasure of ruining them.

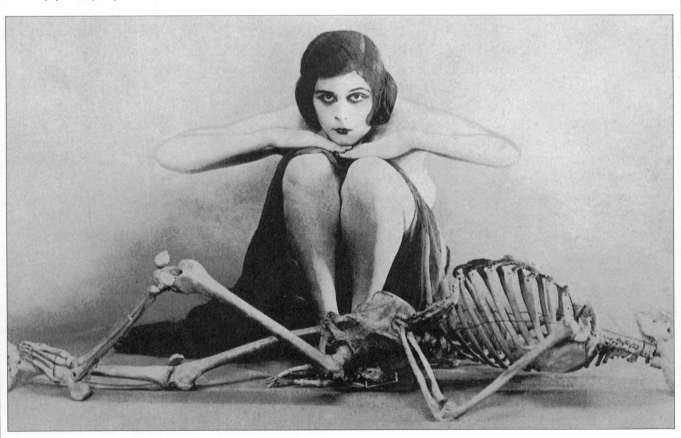

*In a publicity still, the prototypical Hollywood vamp, Theda Bara, crouch-
es like an erotic vulture over the bare bones of a male skeleton—a lurid symbol of
the countless men who fell prey to her wicked wiles.*

born to parents who were themselves illegitimate. It rose from its grave as an alluring young man or woman and swept its prey into orgies that did not stop until the victims died of exhaustion. In many societies, such sexually demanding visitors were blamed for the erotic dreams and nocturnal emissions of males and for the unexplained pregnancies of women thought to be virtuous. Psychologists have drawn a link between the modern fascination with vampirism and some patients' redirection of an adolescent need for love into extreme oral manifestations. Indeed, clinical literature contains numerous cases where actual blood sucking from purposefully inflicted wounds has been integrated with sex or sexual fantasies.

Although Dracula was particularly titillating for repressed Victorians, vampires appear to be no less fascinating in today's relatively permissive social environment. Horror writer Stephen King's *Salem's Lot,* the story of a vampire terrorizing a small town in modern-day Maine, climbed to the top of the best-seller lists in 1976. King got the idea for the novel while he was teaching *Dracula* to a high school English class. Novelist Anne Rice has built a highly successful career on vampires mixed with eroticism in her three best-selling books, *Interview with a Vampire, The Vampire Lestat,* and *Queen of the Damned,* the last of which topped the best-seller list within only a week of its publication in 1988. Hollywood, recognizing a mother lode when it strikes one, has returned again and again to the vampire theme.

Vampires, in short, are popular. Various vampire societies publish journals on the subject, some that are scholarly and others that are decidedly folksy. The Count Dracula Fan Club with headquarters in New York City, for instance, seems to exist mainly so its members can enjoy sharing their interest in the subject. Its newsletter includes recent newspaper articles, poetry, short stories, film and book reviews, and jokes about vampires. But John Vellutini of San Francisco, publisher of the *Journal of Vampirology,* is devoted to serious research, particularly the study of vampirism in Africa, which he says was largely ignored by Montague Summers and later researchers. Vellutini suggests that racism and cultural elitism have contributed to the notion of the eastern European noble as vampire, which has gradually supplanted the historically more accurate idea of vampires springing from peasant stock.

The Los Angeles-based Count Dracula Society, meanwhile, has encouraged serious study of horror films and Gothic literature with a program of annual awards. And while Martin Riccardo's Vampire Studies Society is now inactive and his authoritative quarterly *Journal of Vampirism* is defunct, his Illinois office continues to function as a clearinghouse for information on the subject; Riccardo's *Vampires Unearthed,* a "multi-media bibliography" on Dracula and vampires in general, is considered by many to be the most thorough survey of its kind.

In New York, the Vampire Research Center, founded by self-proclaimed "vampirologist" Stephen Kaplan, maintains a library on the subject, operates a vampirology speakers' bureau, and keeps current Kaplan's vampire census, the only one ever taken. He distributes questionnaires to people who think that they themselves are vampires or who suspect that an acquaintance is. Kaplan then analyzes the returns and interviews the respondents who seem to have made authentic claims. He has said he believes there are 150 to 200 "actual vampires" living in North America today and perhaps 500 throughout the world. Critics contend that Kaplan may be more interested in media attention than in vampires, however, noting that he has appeared on some 1,400 radio and television programs since he took up vampirology.

If so, given the persistence of the public's age-old fascination with the idea of vampires, Kaplan appears to be in a growth industry. The popular image of the vampire, after all, has evolved from the repulsive and truly threatening predator of the sixteenth century to an intriguing and mysterious figure that delights even as it frightens and holds an ever-expanding audience in thrall. Interest in the subject seems unlikely to diminish anytime soon.

ACKNOWLEDGMENTS

The editors wish to express their appreciation to the following individuals and organizations:

François Avril, Department of Manuscripts, Bibliothèque Nationale, Paris, France; Professor Hans Bender, Institut für Grenzgebiete der Psychologie und Psychohygiene, Freiburg, West Germany; Otto Buhbe, Schöppenstedt, West Germany; Professor Diana Buitron, Chevy Chase, Maryland; Roma Chaterjee, New Delhi, India; Volker Dünnhaupt, Bibliothekar, Rheinisches Landesmuseum, Bonn, West Germany; Christiano Felice, Rome, Italy; Leif Geiges, Staufen, West Germany; R. A. Gilbert, Bristol, England; Kenneth Grant, London; Kendall Hopman, Colombo, Sri Lanka; Hungarian National Museum, Budapest, Hungary; Heidi Klein, Bildarchiv Preussischer Kulturbesitz, West Berlin, West Germany; Professor Dimitrios S. Loukatos, Athens, Greece; William McLennan, University of British Columbia, Vancouver, Canada; Raymond McNally, Boston College, Chestnut Hill, Massachusetts; Professor Richard Martin, Princeton University, Princeton, New Jersey; Jeffrey E. Mauger, Curator, The Museum of Native American Cultures, Spokane, Washington; Professor Théodore Monod, Paris, France; Stelios A. Mouzakis, Athens, Greece; Martin Riccardo, Berwyn, Illinois; Professor Robin Riddington, University of British Columbia, Vancouver, Canada; Gabriele Rossi-Osmida, Mirano, Venice; K. W. Sanders, Harzverein für Geschichte und Altertumskunde, Bad Harzburg, West Germany; John Seidensticker, National Zoological Park, Washington, D.C.; Leslie Shepard, Dublin, Ireland; Kostas Spanis, Athens, Greece; Rolf Streichardt, Institut für Grenzgebiete der Psychologie und Psychohygiene, Freiburg, West Germany; Harald Sund, Seattle, Washington; Professor Anthony F. C. Wallace, University of Pennsylvania, Philadelphia, Pennsylvania; Achille Weider, Zurich, Switzerland; Robin K. Wright, Burke Museum, University of Washington, Seattle, Washington.

BIBLIOGRAPHY

Abel, E. L., *Moon Madness*. Greenwich, Conn.: Fawcett, 1976.

Addiss, Stephen, ed., *Japanese Ghosts & Demons: Art of the Supernatural*. New York: George Braziller, 1985.

Armen, Jean-Claude, *Gazelle-Boy*. Transl. by Stephen Hardman. New York: Universe Books, 1974.

Aylesworth, Thomas G., *The Story of Vampires*. New York: McGraw-Hill, 1977.

"Baboon Boy." *Time*, April 1, 1940.

Bagot, Richard, "The Hyenas of Pirra." *Cornhill Magazine*, October 1918.

Bancroft-Hunt, Norman, *People of the Totem*. New York: G. P. Putnam's Sons, 1979.

Barber, Paul, *Vampires, Burial, and Death*. New Haven, Conn.: Yale University Press, 1988.

Baring-Gould, Sabine, *The Book of Were-Wolves*. Detroit: Gale Research, 1973.

Baudez, Claude F., *Central America*. Transl. by James Hogarth. London: Barrie and Jenkins, 1970.

Baumann, Elwood D., *Vampires*. New York: Franklin Watts, 1977.

Benson, Elizabeth P., ed., *Dumbarton Oaks Conference on Olmec*. Washington, D. C.: Dumbarton Oaks Research Library and Collection, 1968.

Bernard, Daniel, and Daniel Dubois, *L'Homme et le Loup*. Paris: Berger-Levrault, 1981.

Bettelheim, Bruno, *The Empty Fortress*. New York: Free Press, 1967.

"Black Magic Casts a Deepening Spell over Troubled Haiti." *Wall Street Journal*, October 20, 1988.

"The Boy Who Thinks He's a Monkey." *Johannesburg Sunday Times* (South Africa), April 11, 1976.

Brandenburg, Jim, *White Wolf: Living with an Arctic Legend*. Ed. by James S. Thornton. Minocqua, Wisc.: NorthWord Press, 1988.

Brown, Joseph Epes, *The Spiritual Legacy of the American Indian*. New York: Crossroad, 1982.

Burger, John R., and Lewis Gardner, *Children of the Wild*. New York: Julian Messner, 1978.

Campbell, Joseph:
Historical Atlas of the World. Vol. 1, Part 1. New York: Harper and Row, 1988.
The Masks of God: Primitive Mythology. New York: Viking Press, 1969.

Carleton, S., "The Wolf." *Pall Mall Magazine*, December 1901.

Copper, Basil, *The Vampire in Legend, Fact and Art*. Secaucus, N.J.: Citadel Press, 1973.

Covarrubias, Miguel, *The Eagle, the Jaquar, and the Serpent*. New York: Alfred A. Knopf, 1954.

Croft, Peter, *Roman Mythology*. London: Octopus Books, 1974.

Dalby, Richard, *Bram Stoker: A Bibliography of First Editions*. London: Dracula Press, 1983.

D'Assier, Adolphe, *Posthumous Humanity: A Study of Phantoms*. Transl. by Henry S. Olcott. London: George Redway, 1887.

Davidson, H. R. Ellis, *Scandinavian Mythology*. New York: Peter Bedrick Books, 1969.

Demaison, André, *Le Livre des Enfants Sauvages*. Paris: André Bonne, 1953.

De Mille, Richard, *Castaneda's Journey*. Santa Barbara, Calif.: Capra Press, 1976.

Drimmer, Frederick, ed., *The Animal Kingdom*. Vol. 1. New York: Greystone Press, 1954.

Duerr, Hans Peter, *Dreamtime*. Transl. by Felicitas Goodman. New York: Basil Blackwell, 1985.

The Editors of Time-Life Books:
Barbarian Tides (TimeFrame series). Alexandria, Va.: Time-Life Books, 1987.
The Indians (The Old West series). New York: Time-Life Books, 1973.

Eisler, Robert, *Man into Wolf: An Anthropological Interpretation of Sadism, Masochism, and Lycanthropy*. London: Routledge and Kegan Paul, 1951.

Evans, E. P., *The Criminal Prosecution and Capital Punishment of Animals*. London: Faber and Faber, 1987 (reprint of 1906 edition).

Farmer, Philip José, ed., *Mother Was a Lovely Beast*. Radnor, Pa.: Chilton, 1974.

Farson, Daniel:
The Man Who Wrote Dracula: A Biography of Bram Stoker. New York: St. Martin's Press, 1975.
Vampires, Zombies, and Monster Men. Garden City, N.Y.: Doubleday, 1976.

Feder, Norman, *American Indian Art*. New York: Harry N. Abrams, 1965.

Ferris, George C., *Sanichar: The Wolf-Boy of India*. New York: G. C. Ferris, 1902.

Fitzhugh, William W., and Aron Crowell, *Crossroads of the Continents*. Washington, D.C.: Smithsonian Institution Press, 1988.

Florescu, Radu, and Raymond T. McNally, *Dracula: A Biography of Vlad the Impaler 1431-1476*. New York: Hawthorn Books, 1973.

Forrest, Earle R., *The Snake Dance of the Hopi Indians*. Los Angeles: Westernlore Press, 1961.

Frazer, James George, *The Golden Bough: A Study in Magic and Religion*. New York: Macmillan, 1951.

Furst, Peter T., and Jill L. Furst, *North American Indian Art*. New York: Rizzoli International, 1982.

Garden, Nancy, *Werewolves*. Philadelphia: J. B. Lippincott, 1973.

Gesell, Arnold, *Wolf Child and Human Child*. New York: Harper & Brothers, 1941.

Gordon, Antoinette K., *Tibetan Religious Art*. New York: Columbia University Press, 1952.

Graves, Robert, *The Greek Myths*. Vol. 1. London: Penguin Books, 1960.

Haining, Peter, *A Dictionary of Ghosts*. London: Robert Hale, 1982.

Haining, Peter, ed., *The Dracula Scrapbook*. London: New English Library, 1976.

Hamel, Frank, *Human Animals: Werewolves & Other Transformations*. New Hyde Park, N.Y.: University Books, 1969.

Hawthorn, Audrey, *Kwakiutl Art*. Seattle, Wash.: University of Washington Press, 1967.

Hendrickson, Robert, *More Cunning than Man: A Social History of Rats and Men*. New York: Stein and Day, 1983.

Hoyt, Olga, *Lust for Blood*. New York: Stein and Day, 1984.

Hurwood, Bernhardt J., *Vampires*. New York: Quick Fox, 1981.

Itard, Jean, *The Wild Boy of Aveyron*. Transl. by Edmund Fawcett, Peter Ayrton, and Joan White. New York: New Left Books, 1972.

Izzard, Sebastian, *Hiroshiqe* (exhibition catalogue). New York: The Ukiyo-e Society of America, 1983.

James, Harry C., *The Hopi Indians: Their History and Their Culture*. Caldwell, Idaho: Caxton Printers, 1956.

Jonaitis, Aldona, *From the Land of the Totem Poles*. New York, N.Y. and Seattle, Wash.: American Museum of Natural History and University of Washington Press, 1988.

Jung, Carl G., et al., *Man and His Symbols*. New York: Doubleday, 1964.

Kaigh, Frederick, *Witchcraft and Magic of Africa*. London: Simson Shand, 1947.

Keithahn, Edward L., *Monuments in Cedar*. Seattle, Wash.: Superior, 1963.

Kelly, I. W., James Rotton, and Roger Culver, "The Moon Was Full and Nothing Happened." *The Skeptical Inquirer*, winter 1985-1986.

King, Francis X., *Witchcraft and Demonology*. New York: Exeter Books, 1987.

Kluckhohn, Clyde, *Navaho Witchcraft*. Boston: Beacon Press, 1967.

Kriss, Marika, *Werewolves, Shapeshifters, and Skinwalkers*. Los Angeles: Shelbourne Press, 1972.

Lane, Harlan, *The Wild Boy of Aveyron*. Cambridge, Mass.: Harvard University Press, 1976.

Lane, Harlan, and Richard Pillard, *The Wild Boy of Burundi*. New York: Random House, 1978.

Leadbeater, C. W., *The Astral Plane: Its Scenery, Inhabitants and Phenomena*. London: Theosophical Publishing Society, 1898.

"Les Malades de Pont-Saint-Esprit Veulent Savoir le Secret de Leur Folie." *Paris Match*, October 27, 1951.

Lieber, Arnold L., and Carolyn R. Sherin, "Homicides and the Lunar Cycle: Towards A Theory of Lunar Influence on Human Emotional Disturbance." *The American Journal of Psychiatry*, July 1972.

Lindskog, Birger, *African Leopard Men*. Uppsala, Sweden: University of Uppsala, 1954.

Lopez, Barry Holstun, *Of Wolves and Men*. New York: Charles Scribner's Sons, 1978.

McHargue, Georgess, *Meet the Werewolf*. Philadelphia: J. B. Lippincott, 1976.

Maclean, Charles, *The Wolf Children*. New York: Hill and Wang, 1978.

McNally, Raymond T.:
Dracula: Prince of Many Faces. Boston: Little, Brown, 1989.
Dracula Was a Woman. New York: McGraw-Hill, 1983.

McNally, Raymond T., comp., *A Clutch of Vampires*. Greenwich, Conn.: New York Graphic Society, 1974.

McNally, Raymond T., and Radu Florescu, *In Search of Dracula: A True History of Dracula and Vampire Legends*. New York: Galahad Books, 1972.

Malin, Edward, *A World of Faces*. Portland, Oreg.: Timber Press, 1978.

Malson, Lucien, *Wolf Children and the Problem of Human Nature*. Transl. by Edmund Fawcett, Peter Ayrton, and Joan White. New York: New Left Books, 1972.

Masters, Anthony, *The Natural History of the Vampire*. New York: G. P. Putnam's Sons, 1972.

Masters, R. E. L., and Jean Houston, *The Varieties of Psychedelic Experience*. London: Turnstone Books, 1966.

Mauger, Jeffrey E., "Art, Masks, and Masking on the Southern Northwest Coast" (essay). Spokane, Wash.: Unpublished, 1988.

Mech, L. David, "Where Can the Wolf Survive?" *National Geographic*, October 1977.

Michell, John, and Robert J. M. Rickard, *Phenomena: A Book of Wonders*. London: Thames and Hudson, 1977.

Mohr, Charles E., *The World of the Bat*. Philadelphia: J. B. Lippincott, 1976.

"Moon Madness." *The Skeptical Inquirer,* summer 1981.

"Moon Madness No Myth." *Science Digest,* March 1981.

Morell, Virginia, "Jungle Rx." *International Wildlife,* May-June 1984.

Morgan, William, *Human-Wolves among the Navaho*. New Haven, Conn.: Yale University Press, 1936.

"Mowgli's Sisters." *Time*, March 3, 1941.

Myles, Douglas, *Prince Dracula: Son of the Devil*. New York: McGraw-Hill, 1988.

Nebesky-Wojkowitz, René de, *Tibetan Religious Dances*. The Hague: Mouton, 1976.

Newman, Bobby, "Scientologists Donating *Dianetics* Edition to Libraries." *The Skeptical Inquirer,* winter 1989.

Newton, Michael, *Monsters, Mysteries and Man*. Reading, Mass.: Addison-Wesley, 1979.

Nicholson, Irene, *Mexican and Central American Mythology*. New York: Peter Bedrick Books, 1985.

O'Donnell, Elliott, *Werewolves*. New York: Longvue Press, 1965.

Ogburn, William F., and Nirmal K. Bose, "On the Trail of the Wolf-Children." *Genetic Psychology Monographs,* August 1959.

Osborne, Harold, *South American Mythology*. London: Hamlyn, 1968.

Otten, Charlotte F., ed., *A Lycanthropy Reader: Werewolves in Western Culture*. Syracuse, N.Y.: Syracuse University Press, 1986.

Park, Edwards, *Treasures of the Smithsonian*. Washington, D. C.: Smithsonian Institution, 1983.

Penrose, Valentine, *The Bloody Countess*. Transl. by Alexander Trocchi. London: Calder & Boyars, 1970.

Perkowski, Jan C., *Vampires of the Slavs*. Cambridge, Mass.: Slavica, 1976.

Piggott, Juliet, *Japanese Mythology*. New York: Peter Bedrick Books, 1969.

Pons, Gregory, "Cornering the Beast." *The Unexplained* (London), Vol. 8, Issue 85.

"The Quest for the Wolf Child." *Sunday Times Colour Magazine* (London), July 30, 1978.

Radin, Paul, *The Trickster: A Study in American Indian Mythology*. London: Routledge and Kegan Paul, 1956.

Ramsey, Jarold, ed. and comp., *Coyote Was Going There: Indian Literature of the Oregon Country*. Seattle, Wash.: University of Washington Press, 1977.

Ray, Dorothy Jean, *Eskimo Masks: Art and Ceremony*. Toronto: McClelland and Stewart, 1967.

Robbins, Rossell Hope, *The Encyclopedia of Witchcraft and Demonology*. New York: Crown, 1959.

Ronay, Gabriel
The Dracula Myth. London: W. H. Allen, 1972.
The Truth about Dracula. New York: Stein and Day, 1972.

Russell, Jeffrey Burton:
A History of Witchcraft: Sorcerers, Heretics and Pagans. London: Thames and Hudson, 1980.
Witchcraft in the Middle Ages. Secaucus, N.J.: Citadel Press, 1972.

Screeton, Paul, "Curse of the Hexham Heads." *The Unexplained* (London), Vol. 10, Issue 117.

Senn, Harry A., *Were-Wolf and Vampire in Romania*. Boulder, Colo.: East European Monographs, 1982.

Shattuck, Roger, *The Forbidden Experiment: The Story of the Wild Boy of Aveyron*. New York: Farrar Straus Giroux, 1980.

Sheaffer, Robert, "News of UFOs, Werewolves, and Loch Ness." *The Skeptical Inquirer,* spring 1988.

Shepard, Leslie A., ed., *Encyclopedia of Occultism & Parapsychology*. Detroit: Gale Research, 1984.

Singh, J. A. L., and Robert M. Zingg, *Wolf-Children and Feral Man*. Hamden, Conn.: Archon Books, 1966.

Smyth, Frank, "The Devil's Scapegoat." *The Unexplained* (London), Vol. 1, Issue 9.

Stoicescu, Nicolae, *Vlad Tepes: Prince of Walachia*. Transl. by Cristina Krikorian. Bucharest: Academy of the Socialist Republic of Romania, 1978.

Stoker, Bram, *Dracula*. New York: Random House, 1897.

Summers, Montague:
The Vampire: His Kith and Kin. New Hyde Park, N.Y.: University Books, 1960.
The Vampire in Europe. Wellingborough, Northamptonshire, England: Aquarian Press, 1980.
The Werewolf. Secaucus, N.J.: Citadel Press, 1966.

Tannahill, Reay, *Flesh and Blood: A History of the Cannibal Complex*. New York: Stein and Day, 1975.

Tripp, Edward, *The Meridian Handbook of Classical Mythology*. New York: New American Library, 1970.

Twitchell, James B., *The Living Dead: A Study of the Vampire in Romantic Literature*. Durham, N.C.: Duke University Press, 1981.

Watson, Peter, "The New 'Wolf Children.'" *Sunday Times* (London), August 26, 1973.

Williman, Daniel, ed., *The Black Death: The Impact of the Fourteenth-Century Plague*. Binghamton, N.Y.: State University of New York, 1982.

Willoughby-Mease, G., *Chinese Ghouls and Goblins*. London: Constable, 1928.

Wolf, Leonard:
A Dream of Dracula: In Search of the Living Dead. Boston: Little, Brown, 1972.
Monsters. San Francisco: Straight Arrow Books, 1974.

Woodward, Ian:
"The Call of the Wild." *The Unexplained* (London), Vol. 4, Issue 39.
The Werewolf Delusion. New York: Paddington Press, 1979.

Wright, Dudley, *The Book of Vampires*. New York: Causeway Books, 1973.

Yalden, D. W., and P. A. Morris, *The Lives of Bats*. New York: New York Times Book Co., 1975.

PICTURE CREDITS

The sources for the illustrations that appear in this book are listed below. Credits from left to right are separated by semicolons, from top to bottom by dashes.

Cover: Art by Bryan Leister. 6, 7: Edward Dossetter, courtesy Department of Library Services, American Museum of Natural History, Neg. No. 44309. 8: Werner Forman Archive, London. 9: Photographs by Stephen Myers, courtesy American Museum of Natural History. 10: Smithsonian Institution, National Museum of Natural History; Lowie Museum of Anthropology, The University of California at Berkeley. 11: Photograph by Stephen Myers, courtesy American Museum of Natural History. 12, 13: Carmelo Guadagno, courtesy the Museum of the American Indian, Heye Foundation, New York City. 14, 15: Photographs by Stephen My

Index

Vampire in Europe, The (Summers), 122
Vampire Lestat, The (Rice), 136
Vampire of Paris. *See* Bertrand, Victor
Vampire Research Center, 136
Vampires: in Africa, 136; of Arabs, 111; and Adolphe d'Assier, 121; in Babylonia, 110; on Bali, *112;* as bats, 109, 134; in Bohemia, 116; in Bulgaria, 113; and Augustin Calmet, 120-121; characteristics of, 113, 117, 133, 135; in China, 110; cholera victims as, *114-115;* and Christianity, 111; deterring of, 112, 113, 116, *119,* 120, 121; eroticism of, 109, 134-136; in films, 109, 136, *137;* in Finland, 113; in folktales, 111, 112, 134; in France, 126-127; in Germany, 127; in Gothic literature, 132-134, 136; in Greece, *110-111,* 112, 113, 134; history of, 109-112; in Hungary, 113, 120-121; and Stephen Kaplan, 136; killing of, 113; and Stephen King, 136; in literature, 109, 132, 136; and Maria Theresa, 121; in Moravia, 121; and plague, 117; and John Polidori, 132-133; popularity of, 136; research on, 136; and Martin Riccardo, 136; and Anne Rice, 136; in Rumania, 113, 134; on Santorini, 112-113; in Serbia, 108, 113; and Bram Stoker, 134; and Montague Summers, 121-123, 127, 130, 135; and Gerard van Swieten, 121; in Transylvania, 111-112, *119;* and John Vellutini, 136; in Yugoslavia, 116-118, 119-120. *See also* Lycanthropy
Vampire Studies Society, 136
Vampires Unearthed (Riccardo), 136
Vampyre, The (Polidori), 132, 133
Varieties of Psychedelic Experience, The (Masters and Houston), 46
Varney the Vampire. 133; illustrations from, *132, 133*
Vellutini, John, and vampires, 136
Verdun, Michel: and Pierre Burgot, 82, 83; crimes of, 83; execution of, 83; trial of, 83; as werewolf, 83
Vereticus (king of Wales), as werewolf, 78
Victor (feral child), *59;* and Jean-Marc Gaspard Itard, 59-60; and Richard Pillard, 68
Vikings, helmet plate of, *36-37*
Vlad II (prince of Walachia), 104
Vlad III (prince of Walachia). *See* Dracula
Vlad Tepes. *See* Dracula
Vlad the Impaler. *See* Dracula
Vrykolkas. See Vampires

W

W, Mr., as werewolf, 91
Wall Street Journal, 24
Walnut brain, defined, 91
Watchmen, defined, 7
Weapons, of leopard-men, *46*
Werewolf Hotline, and werewolves, 72, 91
Werewolf of Ansbach, *84-85*
Werewolf of Caude, 86

Werewolves: and astral projection, 89, 91; in Bavaria, *84-85;* and Henri Bouguet, 88; in Breton, 79; and Robert Burton, 87-88; causes of, 87-88, 89, 91, 93-94; characteristics of, 72-74, 75, 88, 93; and Christianity, 88; in England, 78-79; and Fox Broadcasting Company, 72, 91; in France, 82−87, 88; in Germany, 70−73, *72;* girdle of, 95, *98-99;* and Rose Gladden, 91; history of, 72, 74-75; incantations about, 95, 96, 100, 102; in Ireland, 78, 79; and Charles Webster Leadbeater, 89; in legends, 75-79; and Éliphas Lévi, 88-89; in Lithuania, 75; in Livonia, 75-78; in myths, 74; and out-of-body experiences, 89; in Poland, 75; and porphyria, 93-94; and rabies, 93; research on, 91-93; in romances, 79; salves of, 73-74, 95, *98-99;* and Theosophists, 89; transformation ritual of, 95-103, *96-97, 98-99, 100-101, 102-103;* treatment for, 87; trials of, 82, 83, 86; and Werewolf Hotline, 72, 91; wound doubling of, 75, 89. *See also* Lycanthropy; Transformations; Wolves
Whales, mask of, *15. See also* Sea People
Wild child of Aveyron. *See* Victor (feral child)
William of Newburgh, quoted, 117
Witchcraft and Magic of Africa (Kaigh), 21
Witch doctors, and jackal, 20-21, *22*
Witches: and Francis Bacon, 38; flying of, 38; and Martin Luther, 38; and the Navajo, 43; salves of, 38; and Montague Summers, 122; transformations of, 38-41, *39,* 43; wound doubling of, 38, 41
Wolf charmers, and wolves, *90*
Wolf-child of Hesse, 57
Wolf-children, *56-57, 60-64. See also* Feral children
Wolfhounds, 78
Wolf-land. *See* Ireland
Wolves, *76;* in *Book of the Hunt, 80, 81;* characteristics of, 80-81; consuming of prey by, *77;* and feral children, *56-57,* 60-64; in France, 76, 80, 81; in Germany, *81;* killing by, *77;* mask of, *16;* in North America, 76; and Remus, *56-57, 72;* reputation of, 76; and Romulus, *56-57,* 72; social organization of, 76; as totems, *8;* and wolf charmers, *90. See also* Werewolves
Wound doubling: causes of, 89; defined, 38, 75; and Charles Webster Leadbeater, 89; and Éliphas Lévi, 89; of Margaret Nin-Gilbert, 41; of tricksters, 42; of werewolves, 75, 89; of witches, 38, 41

Y

Yorkshire Ripper, 130
Yugoslavia, vampires in, 116-118, 119-120

Z

Zeus, transformations of, 34, *35*

Time-Life Books Inc.
is a wholly owned subsidiary of
THE TIME INC. BOOK COMPANY

President and Chief Executive Officer: Kelso F. Sutton
President, Time Inc. Books Direct: Christopher T. Linen

TIME-LIFE BOOKS INC.

EDITOR: George Constable
Executive Editor: Ellen Phillips
Director of Design: Louis Klein
Director of Editorial Resources: Phyllis K. Wise
Editorial Board: Russell B. Adams, Jr., Dale M. Brown,
Roberta Conlan, Thomas H. Flaherty, Lee Hassig, Jim
Hicks, Donia Ann Steele, Rosalind Stubenberg
Director of Photography and Research: John Conrad Weiser

PRESIDENT: John M. Fahey, Jr.
Senior Vice Presidents: Robert M. DeSena, James L. Mercer,
Paul R. Stewart, Curtis G. Viebranz, Joseph J. Ward
Vice Presidents: Stephen L. Bair, Stephen L. Goldstein,
Juanita T. James, Andrew P. Kaplan, Susan J. Maruyama,
Robert H. Smith
Supervisor of Quality Control: James King

PUBLISHER: Joseph J. Ward

Editorial Operations
Copy Chief: Diane Ullius
Production: Celia Beattie
Library: Louise D. Forstall

Library of Congress Cataloging-in-Publication Data
Transformations / the editors of Time-Life Books.
p. cm.—(Mysteries of the unknown)
Bibliography: p.
Includes index.
ISBN 0-8094-6364-4. ISBN 0-8094-6365-2 (lib. bdg.)
1. Werewolves. 2. Vampires. 3. Metamorphosis—
Folklore.
I. Time-Life Books. II. Series.
GR830.W4T73 1989   89-20150
398'.469—dc20   CIP

MYSTERIES OF THE UNKNOWN

SERIES DIRECTOR: Jim Hicks
Series Administrator: Myrna Traylor-Herndon
Designer: Herbert H. Quarmby

Editorial Staff for *Transformations*
Associate Editor: Susan Kelly (pictures)
Text Editors: Dale M. Brown, Janet Cave, Robert Doyle
Researchers: Sharon Obermiller (lead research), Sarah
Ince, Philip M. Murphy, Elizabeth D. Ward
Staff Writers: Marfé Ferguson Delano, Margery duMond
Assistant Designer: Susan M. Gibas
Copy Coordinators: Mary Beth Oelkers-Keegan,
Jarelle S. Stein
Picture Coordinators: Katherine L. Griffin, Ruth J. Moss
Editorial Assistant: Donna Fountain

Special Contributors: Lesley Coleman, Christine Hinze
(London, picture research); Patricia A. Paterno, Evelyn S.
Prettyman, Pamela Whitney (research); Ann Bradley,
David Mazie, Daniel Stashower, John R. Sullivan,
Ricardo Villanueva (text); John Drummond (design);
Hazel Blumberg-McKee (index)

Correspondents: Elisabeth Kraemer-Singh (Bonn), Vanessa
Kramer (London), Christina Lieberman (New York), Maria
Vincenza Aloisi (Paris), Ann Natanson (Rome)
Valuable assistance was also provided by Mirka Gondicas
(Athens); Brigid Grauman (Brussels); Susan Viets (Buda-
pest); Bing Wong (Hong Kong); Marlin Levin (Jerusalem);
Martha de la Cal (Lisbon); Judy Aspinall (London); Trini
Bandrés (Madrid); Felix Rosenthal (Moscow); Simmi
Dhanda, Deepak Puri (New Delhi); Elizabeth Brown (New
York); John Maier (Rio); Ann Wise (Rome); Dick Berry
(Tokyo); Traudl Lessing (Vienna).

Consultant:
Marcello Truzzi, professor of sociology at Eastern Michi-
gan University, is also director of the Center for Scientific
Anomalies Research (CSAR) and editor of its journal, the
Zetetic Scholar. Dr. Truzzi, who considers himself a "con-
structive skeptic" with regard to claims of the paranormal, works through the CSAR to produce dialogues between critics and proponents of unusual scientific claims.

Other Publications:

TIME-LIFE LIBRARY OF CURIOUS AND UNUSUAL FACTS
AMERICAN COUNTRY
VOYAGE THROUGH THE UNIVERSE
THE THIRD REICH
THE TIME-LIFE GARDENER'S GUIDE
TIME FRAME
FIX IT YOURSELF
FITNESS, HEALTH & NUTRITION
SUCCESSFUL PARENTING
HEALTHY HOME COOKING
UNDERSTANDING COMPUTERS
LIBRARY OF NATIONS
THE ENCHANTED WORLD
THE KODAK LIBRARY OF CREATIVE PHOTOGRAPHY
GREAT MEALS IN MINUTES
THE CIVIL WAR
PLANET EARTH
COLLECTOR'S LIBRARY OF THE CIVIL WAR
THE EPIC OF FLIGHT
THE GOOD COOK
WORLD WAR II
HOME REPAIR AND IMPROVEMENT
THE OLD WEST

*For information on and a full description of any of the Time-
Life Books series listed above, please call 1-800-621-7026 or
write:*
Reader Information
Time-Life Customer Service
P.O. Box C-32068
Richmond, Virginia 23261-2068

This volume is one of a series that examines the history
and nature of seemingly paranormal phenomena. Other
books in the series include: